Buddhism and Socio-Economic Life of Eastern India

Reconstructing Indian History & Culture, no. 9

Buddhism and Socio-Economic Life of Eastern India

with special reference to Bengal and Orissa
(8th — 12th Centuries AD)

Bimal Chandra Mohapatra

D.K. Printworld (P) Ltd.
NEW DELHI-110015

Cataloging in Publication Data — DK

Mohapatra, Bimal Chandra, 1962-
Buddhism and socio-economic life of eastern India.
(Reconstructing Indian history & culture; no. 9).
Includes bibliographical references (p.).
Includes index.

1. Buddhism -- India -- Bengal. 2. Buddhism -- India -- Orissa. 3. Bengal (India) -- Social conditions. 4. Orissa (India) -- Social conditions. 5. Bengal (India) -- Economic conditions. 6. Orissa (India) -- Economic conditions. 7. Bengal (India) -- History. 8. Orissa (India) -- History. I. Title. II. Series: Reconstructing Indian history & culture; no. 9.

ISBN 81-246-0055-4

First Published in India in 1995

Printed and Published by:
D.K. Printworld (P) Ltd.
Regd. office : 'Sri Kunj', F-52, Bali Nagar
New Delhi - 110015
Phone : (011) 546-6019; *Fax* : (011) 546-5926

To
my beloved parents

Preface

THIS book aims at presenting a comprehensive discussion about the condition of Buddhism and its impact on the social and economic conditions of Bengal and Orissa from the eighth to twelfth century AD. The study has been restricted to two dominating dynasties of Bengal and Orissa who were great patrons of Buddhism namely the Pālas of Bengal (present Bengal, Bihar and Bangladesh) who ruled from eighth to twelfth century AD and the Bhaumakaras of Orissa who ruled from eighth to tenth century AD.

It is significant to note that when Buddhism was declining and Brāhmaṇism was in a very affluent condition throughout India, the eastern part of India, particularly Bengal (present Bengal, Bihar and Bangladesh) and Orissa, rendered a great impetus to Buddhism in the period from eighth to twelfth century AD. This book discusses in details the condition of Buddhism and its impact on the socio-economic condition of Bengal and Orissa during that period.

Although much work has been done on the religion, society and economic conditions of this period in Bengal and Orissa, but the relationship between the religion and socio-economic life of the people in this area has not been done so far. An effort has been made to fill this gap. We know that Buddhism had a meaningful relation to society and economy, helping the evolution of new patterns of social and economic behaviour and attitude . I have tried to look into this aspect of religion through this book.

The methodology adopted in this study is analytical as well as comparative. It has been tried to make the analysis as objective as possible.

I take this opportunity to express my gratitude to all those who have helped me to complete this task through their generous cooperation.

No amount of word can adequately convey my sense of gratitude to Dr. (Miss) Sudha Sengupta, retired associate professor, Department of Buddhist Studies, University of Delhi as without her invaluable guidance, motherly affection and constant inspiration the present work would not have been possible.

I am highly indebted to Prof. Mahesh Tiwari, Prof. K.K. Mittal, Prof. Sanghasen Singh, and Dr. K.T.S. Sarao of the Deptt. of Buddhist Studies, University of Delhi and Prof. K.S. Behera, Deptt. of History, Utkal University and Prof. P.K. Mishra, Deptt. of History, Sambalpur University for their kind cooperation and encouragement.

I would like to gratefully acknowledge my indebtedness to my parents and other family members, but for whose care, affection and cooperation, it would have been difficult for me to complete this work. No word of appreciation would suffice to record my debt to my wife for her perennial love, support and understanding. I am immensely thankful to all my friends for their constant inspiration.

My thanks are due to the Archaeological Survey of India, New Delhi and National Museum, New Delhi for generously providing me the necessary photographs for this book.

Last but not the least, I sincerely appreciate the highly strenuous and valuable task undertaken by Mr. Susheel K. Mittal of D.K. Printworld for publication of the book.

Bimal Chandra Mohapatra

Contents

Abbreviations

AAI	*Art and Architecture of India* by Benjamin Rowland
AIE	*Ancient Indian Education* by R.K. Mookerji
AO	*Acta Orientalia*
ASB	Asiatic Society of Bengal
ASI	Archaeological Survey of India
ASR	*Archaeological Survey of India, Reports*
BI	*Bibliotheca Indica* series of the Asiatic Society, Calcutta
Ch.	Chapter
CII	*Corpus Inscriptionum Indicarum*
CP	Copper Plate
CR	*Calcutta Review*
DPC	Dabiprasad Chattopadhyah
EC	*Epigraphia Carnatica*
Ed.	Edited by
EHB	*Early History of Bengal* by P.L. Paul
EHNI	*Early History of North India* by S. Chattopadhyay
EI	*Epigraphica Indica*
EIBO	*Early Inscriptions of Bihar and Orissa*
Fig.	Figure

GL	*Gauda-lekhamālā* by A.K. Maitreya
HAB	*History of Ancient Bengal* by R.C. Majumdar
HBR	*History of Bengal*, ed. by R.C. Majumdar
HCIP	*History and Culture of the Indian People*
IA	*Indian Antiquary*
IB	*Inscriptions of Bengal* by N.G. Majumdar
IC	*Indian Culture*
IHQ	*Indian Historical Quarterly*
IO	*Inscriptions of Orissa*
JA	*Journal Asiatique*
JAHRS	*Journal of the Andhra Historical Research Society*
JAIH	*Journal of Ancient Indian History*
JARS	*Journal of the Assam Research Society*
JAS	*Journal of the Asiatic Society*
JASB	*Journal of the Asiatic Society of Bengal*
JASL	*Journal of the Asiatic Society, Letters*
JBORS	*Journal of the Bihar and Orissa Research Society*
JBRS	*Journal of Bihar Research Society*
JBTS	*Journal of the Buddhist Text Society*
JIH	*Journal of Indian History*
JKHRS	*Journal of the Kalinga Historical Research Society*
JNSI	*Journal of the Numismatic Society of India*
JOA	*Journal of Orissa Academy*
JOR	*Journal of Oriental Research*
JRAS	*Journal of the Royal Asiatic Society of Great Britain and Ireland*

JRASB	*Journal of the Royal Asiatic Society of Bengal*
JRASBL	*Journal of the Royal Asiatic Society of Bengal, Letters*
JRSA	*Journal of the Royal Society of Arts*
MASB	*Memoirs of the Asiastic Society of Bengal*
MASI	*Memoirs of Archaeological Survey of India*
MR	*Modern Review*
NS	New Series
OHRJ	*Orissa Historical Research Journal*
ORC	Obscure Religious cults
PAIOC	*Proceedings of the All India Oriental Conference*
PASB	*Proceedings of the Asiatic Society of Bengal*
PB	*Pālas of Bengal* by R.D. Banerji
PIHC	*Proceedings of Indian History Congress*
Pl.	Plate
RE	Rock Edict
RC	*Rāmacarita*
SBE	*Sacred Books of the East*
SBH	*Sacred Books of the Hindus*
SI	*Select Inscriptions* by D.C. Sircar

List of Illustrations

Orissa

During the Bhaumakara period (8th-10th century AD)

10. Bust of Buddha, stone, 15 cm, Ratnagiri, Orissa; National Museum, Delhi.
11. Buddha in *Bhūmisparśa Mudrā*, stone, 28 cm, Ratnagiri, Orissa; National Museum, Delhi.
12. Buddha in *Dhyāna Mudrā*, stone, 28 cm, Ratnagiri, Orissa; National Museum, Delhi.

Bengal and Bihar
During the Pāla period
(8th-12th century AD)

13. Māyādevī, Birth of Buddha, stone, 14 cm, Nalanda, Bihar; Indian Museum, Calcutta.
14. Crowned Buddha, Bihar; Indian Museum, Calcutta.
15. Tārā, Bodh Gaya, Bihar; Indian Museum, Calcutta.
16. Tārā, Bihar; Indian Museum, Calcutta.
17. Some Aspects of Buddha's life, Bihar; Indian Museum, Calcutta.
18. Buddha in Preaching pose, 51 cm, Eastern India; National Museum, Delhi.
19. *Aṣṭa Mahābodhisattvas*, 19.5 cm. Bengal; National Museum, Delhi.
20. *Dhyānī* Buddha, 19.5 cm. Bihar; National Museum, Delhi.
21. Buddha Panel, stone, 30cm, Bengal; National Museum, Delhi.

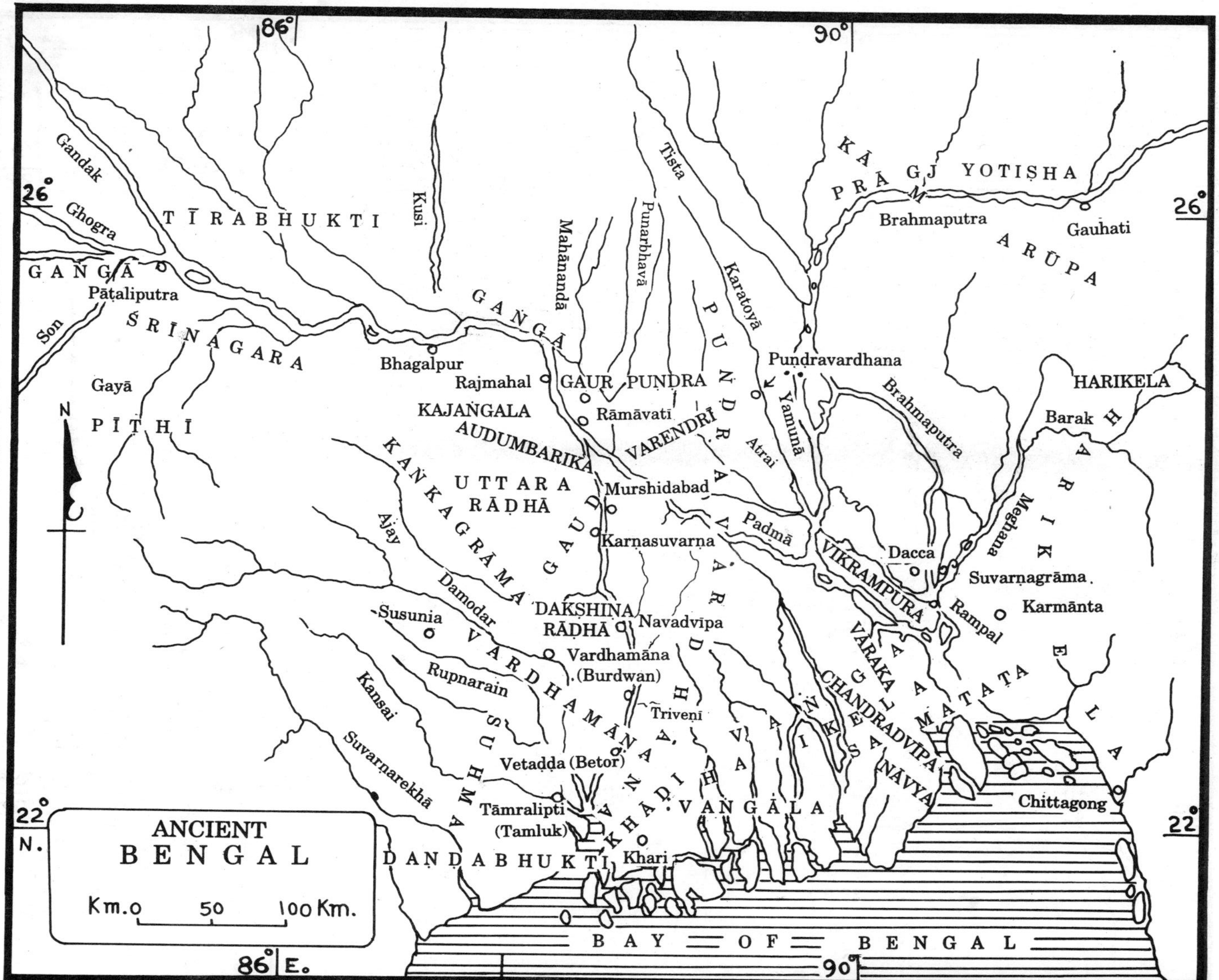
ANCIENT
BENGAL
Km.0 50 100 Km.
N
26°
22° N.
86°
86° E.
90°
22°
26°
TĪRABHUKTI
GAṄGĀ
Gandak
Ghogra
Son
Pāṭaliputra
ŚRĪNAGARA
Gayā
PĪṬHĪ
Kusi
Bhagalpur
Rajmahal
KAJAṄGALA
AUDUMBARIKA
KAṄKAGRĀMA
UTTARA RĀḌHĀ
GAUḌA
DAKSHINA RĀḌHĀ
VARDHAMĀNA
SUHMA
DAṆḌABHUKTI
Ajay
Damodar
Susunia
Rupnarain
Kansai
Suvarṇarekhā
Vetaḍḍa (Betor)
Tāmralipti (Tamluk)
Khari
KHĀḌI
VAṄGĀLA
Vardhamāna (Burdwan)
Triveṇī
Navadvīpa
Karṇasuvarṇa
Murshidabad
Mahānandā
Punarbhavā
GAUR PUNDRA
Rāmāvatī
VARENDRĪ
PUṆḌRAVARDHANA
Tista
Karatoyā
Atrai
Yamunā
Pundravardhana
Padmā
Brahmaputra
PRĀGJYOTISHA
KĀMARŪPA
Gauhati
HARIKELA
Barak
Meghana
Dacca
VIKRAMPURA
Suvarṇagrāma
Karmānta
Rampal
VĀRAKA
SAMATAṬA
CHANDRADVĪPA
NĀVYA
VAṄGĀLA
Chittagong
BAY OF BENGAL

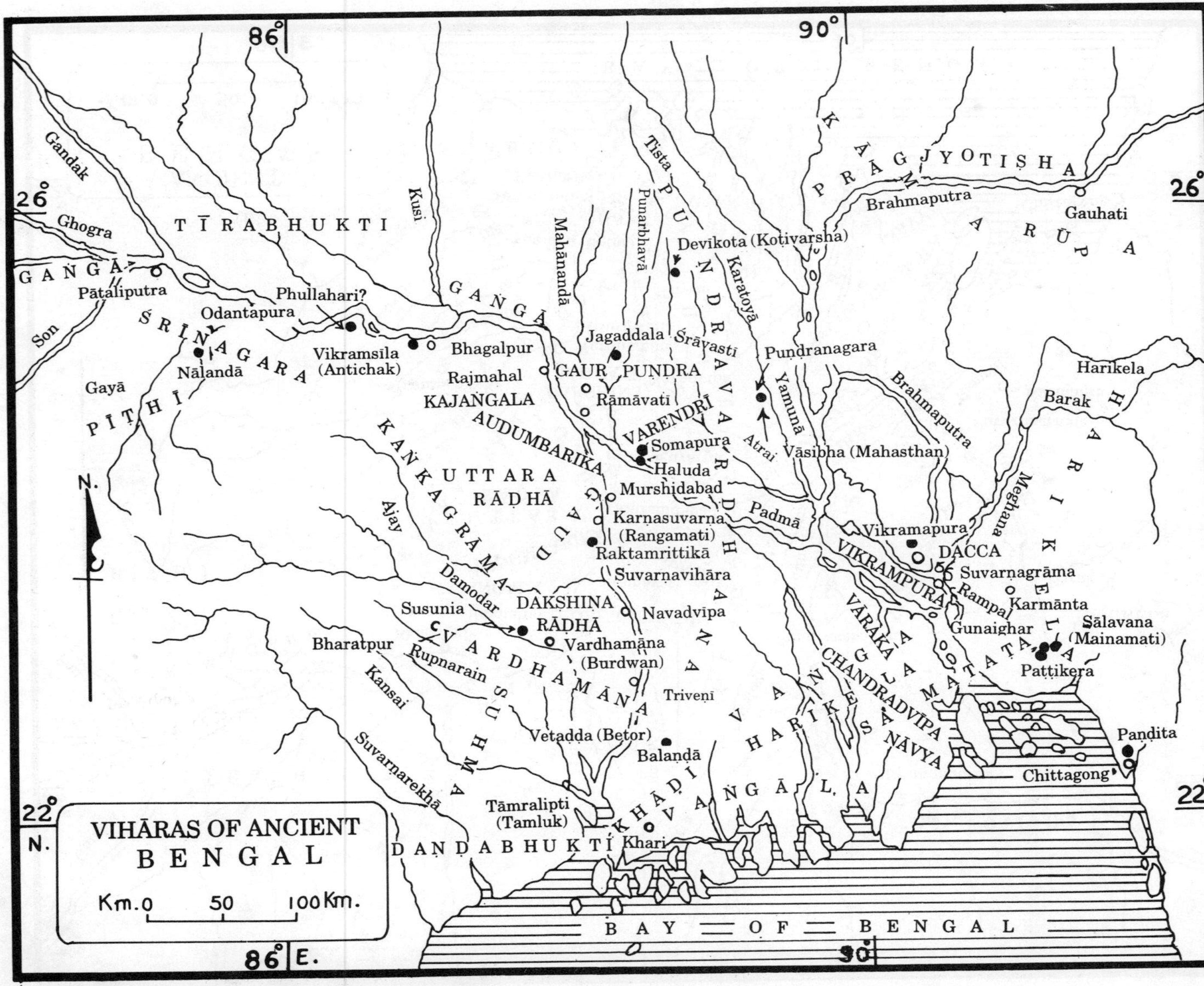
VIHĀRAS OF ANCIENT
BENGAL
Km.0 50 100Km.
86° 90° 26° 22° N. 86° E. 90°
TĪRABHUKTI
PRĀGJYOTISHA
KĀMARŪPA
PUṆḌRAVARDHANA
HARIKELA
GAṄGĀ
ŚRĪNAGARA
PĪṬHĪ
KAJAṄGALA
AUDUMBARIKA
KAṄKAGRĀMA
UTTARA RĀḌHĀ
DAKSHIṆA RĀḌHĀ
VARDHAMĀNA
SUHMA
DAṆḌABHUKTĪ
KHAḌĪ
VAṄGĀLA
HARIKELA
VAṄGA
SAMATAṬA
VĀRAKA
CHANDRADVĪPA
NĀVYA
VIKRAMPURA
VARENDRĪ
GAUḌA
BAY OF BENGAL
Gandak
Ghogra
Son
Kusi
Mahānandā
Punarbhavā
Tista
Karatoyā
Yamunā
Atrai
Padmā
Brahmaputra
Meghana
Barak
Ajay
Damodar
Rupnarain
Kansai
Suvarṇarekhā
Pāṭaliputra
Nālandā
Gayā
Odantapura
Phullahari?
Vikramsīla (Antichak)
Bhagalpur
Rajmahal
GAUR
PUṆḌRA
Jagaddala
Śrāvasti
Rāmāvatī
Devīkota (Koṭivarsha)
Puṇḍranagara
Vāsibha (Mahasthan)
Somapura
Haluda
Murshidabad
Karṇasuvarṇa (Rangamati)
Raktamrittikā
Suvarṇavihāra
Navadvīpa
Susunia
Bharatpur
Vardhamāna (Burdwan)
Triveṇī
Vetadda (Betor)
Balandā
Tāmralipti (Tamluk)
Khari
Vikramapura
DACCA
Suvarṇagrāma
Rampal
Karmānta
Gunaighar
Sālavana (Mainamati)
Paṭṭikera
Paṇḍita
Chittagong
Gauhati
Harikela

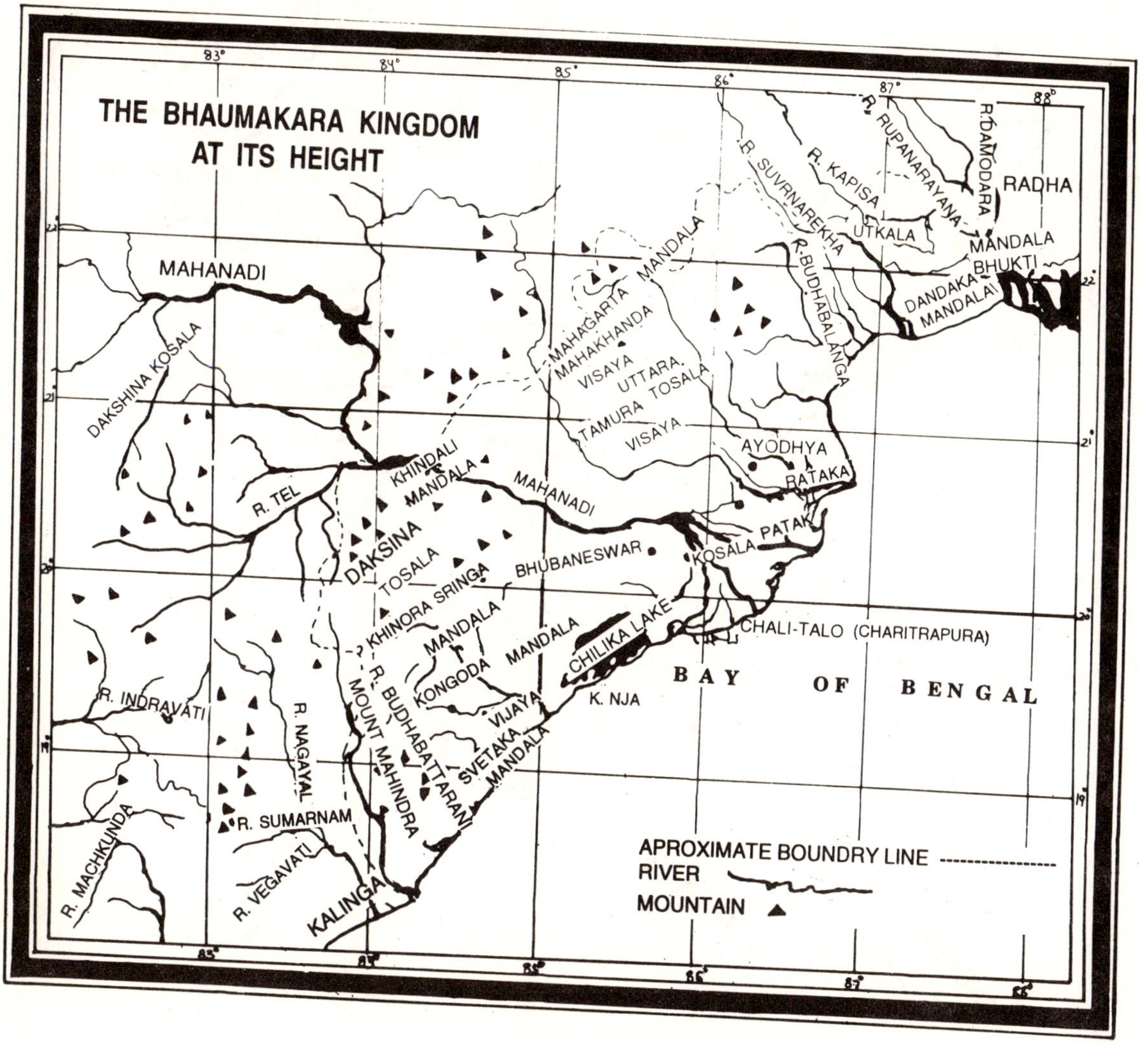

THE BHAUMAKARA KINGDOM
AT ITS HEIGHT
MAHANADI
DAKSHINA KOSALA
R. TEL
KHINDALI MANDALA
DAKSINA TOSALA
KHINORA SRINGA MANDALA
KONGODA MANDALA
MAHAGARTA MANDALA
MAHAKHANDA VISAYA
UTTARA TOSALA
TAMURA VISAYA
BHUBANESWAR
AYODHYA
RATAKA
KOSALA PATAK
CHILIKA LAKE
CHALI-TALO (CHARITRAPURA)
BAY OF BENGAL
K. NJA
VIJAYA
SVETAKA MANDALA
R. BUDHABATARANI
MOUNT MAHINDRA
R. INDRAVATI
R. NAGAYAL
R. SUMARNAM
R. MACHKUNDA
R. VEGAVATI
KALINGA
R. SUVRNAREKHA
R. BUDHABALANGA
R. KAPISA
R. RUPANARAYANA
R. DAMODARA
RADHA
UTKALA
MANDALA
BHUKTI
DANDAKA MANDALA
APROXIMATE BOUNDRY LINE
RIVER
MOUNTAIN

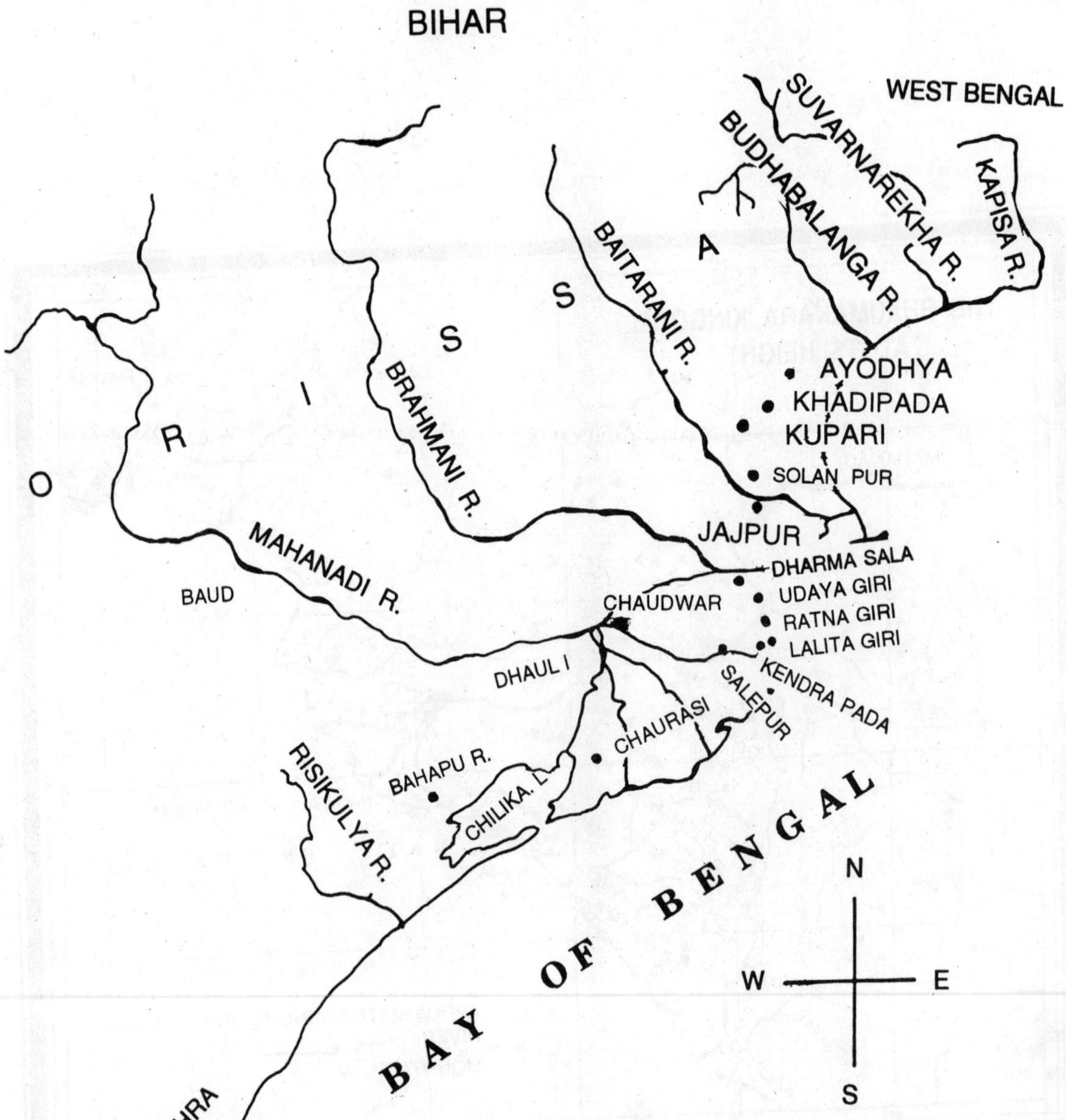

BUDDHIST CENTRES
IN ORISSA DURING
BHAUMAKARA PERIOD

1

Introduction

THE period from the eighth to twelfth century AD was significant from many points as far as Buddhism is concerned in eastern part of India. This period saw the last glory of the Buddhists in Indiaand there was a total transformation in the social and economic relations. It was the period when feudalism was raising its head in Bengal and Orissa and there was great transformation in the Buddhist faith also. Thus this period was a transitional one from ancient to medieval period which witnessed many changes in the society, economic conditions and religious faiths in Bengal and Orissa.

This work is based mainly on original sources though several secondary sources have also been consulted. We now discuss in detail about the sources which are given in two separate sections, one dealing with the sources for the history of Bengal during the rule of the Pālas, another for the history of Orissa during the rule of the Bhaumakaras.

SOURCES

Bengal under the Pālas

The sources of the history of ancient Bengal are of two broad categories, archaeological and literary. Epigraphical, numismatic and monumental records constitute the epigraphic source. The inscriptions found on stones or metals have been found in various places and they provide us a lot of informations about the period under study. The Pāla monarchs were famous for issuing many land grants with inscriptions which describe them as devout Buddhists. These land grants also indicate the extent and the nature of patronage given to Buddhism by the Pāla monarchs. At the same time these inscriptions proved the catholicity of the Pāla monarchs towards other religious sects. The role played by Bengal in the international sphere of Buddhism is obtained from these records. These epigraphic records provide us concrete informations about the social conditions and economic activities of the people of the contemporary period.

Numismatic source, i.e., coins and seals does not constitute a major source so far as Bengal of our period is concerned, since the Pālas are not known to have issued any coin. The informations provided by some seals have ascertained the sites of the Buddhist Universities of Nālandā and Somapura.

The ruins of different Buddhist Monasteries like Nālandā and Somapura, stand silent witness to the flourishing condition of Buddhism under the Pālas. The metal and stone images belonging to various sects of Buddhism discovered from various places in Bengal and Bihar (ancient Bengal) speak of the popularity of Buddhism. The affinity between Bengal and several south-east Asian sculptures has been established because of these monuments.

Literary source, though sometimes corroborative in nature is of immense value to us. This source is divided into two categories, indigenous and foreign. Indigenous primary texts which are mostly written in Sanskrit give us valuable information about the history of Bengal. The foreign texts, particularly Chinese, Napalese and Tibetan provide us informations about the evolution of Buddhism in Bengal. The discovery of a large number of manuscripts from Nepal have enriched our knowledge about the offshoots of Mahāyāna Buddhism like Sahajayāna and Kālacakrayāna. Tibetan texts have informed us about many Buddhist centres in Bengal like Nālandā, Vikramaśilā, Somapura, Jagaddalā, Devīkoṭa and many others. The condition of Buddhism in the pre-Pāla period has been known to us because of the Chinese travelogues of Fahien,

Hiuen Tsang and T-tsang.

Lama Tāranāth's *History of Buddhism in India* gives not only detailed account of the condition of Buddhism in Bengal but also the history of the Pāla rulers in Bengal. In spite of some discrepancies, we must admit that Tāranāth had access to some historical texts, now lost to us and did not draw purely on his imagination. Tāranāth gathered his informations from certain old texts and either these were wrong in many details or he misunderstood them.

Another important literary source is the *Subhāṣitaratnakośa*, an anthology of Sanskrit poems compiled by a Buddhist scholar named Vidyākara in AD 1100. This book gives us a view of the village life in the early medieval Bengal. It begins with verses in praise of the Buddha followed by verses on the other Buddhist deities as well as brāhmaṇical gods and goddesses which is an evidence of the catholic spirit towards religions. The verses are on seasons, periods of human life, love, goodmen, villains, poverty and praise of kings. Thus it served as an important source for getting a good knowledge about the village life in the early medieval Bengal.

In the course of preparation of this work all possible sources including epigraphic records, archaeological monuments, and literary texts belonging to our period of investigation have been consulted.

Orissa under the Bhaumakaras

The present work has been constructed mainly on the basis of primary sources. The primary sources include epigraphic, archaeological findings and literature. We are lucky enough to get as many as twenty-four epigraphic records from the period of the Bhaumakara which include nineteen copper-plate inscriptions and five stone inscriptions. The copper-plate grants were donations of different rulers. Inscriptions are engraved in Sanskrit language on single copper-plates. The texts of these inscriptions are composed both in prose and verse which follow a definite order. The opening is an innovation to a deity, then follows the names and achievements of the donor and his ancestors. Thereafter comes an address of the ruler to officers and feudatories. Then comes the statement on the donee and his ancestors which is then followed by a description of the object of donation. The record concludes with an implication on anyone who may disturb the charity and with a praise on anyone who may honour the same. These inscriptions throw a flood of light on the social conditions, administrative organisations, economic condition and above all the religious conditions prevailing at that time.

The inscriptions of the feudatories of the Bhauma kings like Sulkis, Tuṅgas, Gaṅgas of Svetaka, Bhañjas of Khiñjali Maṇḍala and Nalas provide us information about the social, economic and religious conditions of that period. Some Bhauma contemporary records like the Rāṣṭrakūṭas, the Pālas provide us valuable informations.

Like Bengal, in Orissa also coins do not constitute a source of our study as there is no evidence of issuing coins by the rulers of Orissa during this period.

The excavations at various places in Orissa provide us a lot of information, so far as study of ancient Orissan history is concerned. The excavations have exposed various types of monuments, i.e., images, monasteries, *stūpa*s etc. which are of greater value than epigraphic records.

There is an initial difficulty in utilising the old literature because of two names Oḍra and Utkala, which are generally recognised to be the old designations of Orissa. The *Purāṇa*s which provide some reference to Orissa are the *Viṣṇu Purāṇa*, the *Harivaṁśa Purāṇa*, and the *Matsya Purāṇa*. The Oriya *Mahābhārata* of Sāralā Das and the *Bhakti Bhāgavata Mahākāvya* of Kavi Ḍinḍima Jiva Devācārya are very important source for this work. Another very interesting and major source of our information is the Mādalā Pāñji, a chronicle of political history of the Jagannāth Temple at Purī. Beginning from the *Satyayuga*, these chronicles record year by year, and every day-by-day, every important events that happened in Orissa in connection with the famous image of Jagannāth at Purī. Though the composition is full of fanciful and imaginary stories, still it provides some knowledge about the contemporary history of Orissa.

Foreign accounts also play a major role in providing informations for our work. Lama Tāranāth's *History of Buddhism in India*, translated by

Lama Chimpa and Alka Chattopadhyaya and edited by D.P. Chatopadhyaya is a very important source. The Ceylonese chronicle the *Daṭhavaṁsa* edited by Dr. B.C. Law, provides informations for this work. The acocunts of Chinese traveller Fa-hien and Hiuen-Tsang are also utilised for this work. There is a very interesting reference to Orissa in a Chinese historical chronicle brought to light by Sylvan Levi. It records the fact that in AD 795 a king of Wu-cha (Uḍra of Orissa) sent an autographed Buddhist manuscript to the Chinese emperor Ta-tsang. The value of this statement in fixing the chronology of the kings of the Bhauma dynasty is very great.

In the ninth and tenth centuries AD, some Arab and Persian travellers visited different parts of India including Orissa and they left valuable accounts of Orissa. Ibn Khurdadhbih, an Arab geographer referred to a place Urishin, situated on the eastern coast of India. This place has been identified as Orissa.[1] The work of the traveller Abu Abdillah Iban Ishaq was the source of information for Ibn Khurdadhbih's geography which refers to a woman, who ruled over Orissa. Taking the intitial year of the Bhauma era as AD 736, we have seen that Bhauma queen Tribhuvana Mahādevī was ruling over Orissa in AD 846. Since Ibn Khurdadhbih completed the first draft in AD 846, there can be no doubt that his accounts refer to the Bhauma kingdom of Orissa during the reign of Tibhuvana Mahādevī.[2] Ibn Rusta, another Arab geographer, mentions the Ursfin and its queen Rubiya. He completed his work in AD 920 and would therefore be a close contemporary of the Bhauma Queen Daṇḍi Mahādevī of Orissa who was ruling between AD 916 and 923.

After discussing about the sources, we now discuss in the following pages about the historical background of the two dominant dynasties of the period of our study, i.e., the Pālas of Bengal and the Bhaumakaras of Orissa.

HISTORICAL BACKGROUND

Pālas of Bengal

The contemporary records describe the political condition of Bengal in the middle of the eighth century AD as *Mastyanyāya*,[3] a technical term used in treaties on politics to denote the absence of a central ruling authority resulting in a chaotic state, where every loyal chief assumes royal authority and might alone is right. This state of political disintegration was caused by the series of foreign invasions and the successive changes of ruling dynasties in Gauḍa and Vaṅga regions of Bengal. Thus Bengal suffered a great political uncertainty.

A new epoch in the history of Bengal was marked with the foundation of the Pāla dynasty about the middle of the eighth century AD. The anarchy and confusion which prevailed in Bengal for more than a century had made people suffer from untold miseries for a long period. The people suddenly showed a great spirit of political wisdom to which there is no recorded parallel in the history of Bengal. They thought it well that the establishment of a single-strong central authority offered the only effective remedy against political disintegration within and invasions from abroad. They must have realised that a happy state of thing could be achieved only if all the authority would be surrended to one person. In order to achieve a greater aim, some personal sacrifice was to be made. This feeling made the petty chiefs determined to surrender their authority to one person, who could in return safeguard the interests of their kingdoms and their people. This sacrifice of individual interests for a national cause was itself a great achievement at the eighth century AD. Thus without any struggle the independent political chiefs recognised the suzerainty of a popular hero named Gopāla. Unfortunately this historic event in the history of Bengal is not described in detail. Only one inscription of the Pāla period, i.e., the Khālimpur copper-plate of Dharmapāla refers to this event. The translation of the paragraph of Khālimpur copper-plate which refers to this event is as follows : "His son was the crest jewel of the heads of kings, the glorious Gopāla, whom the people made take the hand of Forture, to put an end to the practice of fishes".[4]

In a footnote to the above, Keilhorn adds, "Gopāla was made King by the people to put an end to a lawless state of things in which everyone was the prey of his neighbour".[5]

There was no dispute regarding Gopāla's becoming king of Bengal to put an end to the state of anarchy which prevailed in Bengal. The point of debate is the agency that made him king. There was a term *prakṛtis* in the Khālimpur copper-plate, referred above, which means subjects.[6] It has been held commonly that Gopāla was elected king by the general body of people. It would, perhaps, be more reasonable to hold that the choice was originally made by the leading chiefs and was subsequently endorsed and acclaimed by the people.[7]

We have very little information about the life and reign of Gopāla, the first king of the Pāla dynasty in Bengal. The official records of the Pālas refer in general terms about Gopāla's father Vapyata and grandfather Dayitavishnu. There is no evidence to prove that the forefathers of Gopāla were ruling chiefs. Gopāla was described as *Rājabhatādi-Vaṁsa-Patita* in the commentary to *Aṣṭasāhasrika Prajñāpāramitā*, composed by Haribhadra. From this, H.P. Sastri concludes that Dharmapāla, the son and successor of Gopāla belonged to the family of a military officer of some king.[8]

We have very scanty information about the origin of the royal Pāla family. Pāla inscriptions were silent about their origin. According to the Kamauli plate of Vaidyadeva, who was a minister of a Pāla king, Vigrahapāla III is said to be have belonged to the solar dynasty.[9] According to the commentary of Sandhyākara Nandi's *Rāmcarita*, Dharmapāla was 'the light of *samudra*'s race, i.e., descended from the Ocean.[10] As these two records belong to a period more than 300 years after the accession of Gopāla, it seems unbelievable. As Bengali text *Dharma-Maṅgala*, composed by Ghanarāma[11] records that Dharmapāla had no son and his queen Vallabhadevī was banished to a forest. There she had a liaison with the ocean and a son was born to her. This story has no relevance for us because of lack of concrete evidence. As to the caste of the Pālas, the commentary on a verse of *Rāmcarita*[12] says that Rāmapāla was born of a kṣatriya king. Tāranātha[13] gives us information that Gopāla was begotten on a kṣatriya woman by the Tree-God. We have evidences about the Pāla dynasty's matrimonial contacts with the other kṣatriya dynasties like the Rāṣṭrakūṭas and the Kālacūris. All these facts make us believe that the Pālas, like most of the ruling families in that period, were regarded as kṣatriyas.

It is very different to find out the reasons behind the silence of the Pāla records about their origin or caste. It is perhaps due to the influence of Buddhism on the Pāla monarchs, as Buddhism does not recognise any caste. The copper-plates of the Pālas begin with an invocation to Lord Buddha, and many kings of the dynasty are known to have been great patrons of Buddhism.

EXTENT OF THE KINGDOM

There is uncertainty over the location of the original kingdom of Gopāla. The fact that during the first two hundred years of the Pāla rule, covering the reigns of eight kings, almost all the copper-plate grants were issued from Victorious camps in Magadha, and all the other inscriptions, with only a single exception, belonged to that region, naturally led many to conclude that the Pālas originally ruled in Magadha and subsequently conquered Bengal. But this view is not acceptable to us because the *Rāmacarita*[14] refers to Varendri as the *Janakabhuh* or ancenstral home of the Pālas. The Bādāl Pillar inscription[15] says that Dharmapāla to begin with, was only the ruler of the east and gradually spread his dominions, in other directions.

It may be believed that the Pālas were originally the rulers of Vaṅga and the name came to be applied to the rest of the Bengal province with the growth of their dominions.

During the course of Pāla rule the extent of the kingdom varied from time to time. Gauḍa, Vaṅga, Samataṭa, Harikela, Candradvīpa, Vaṅgāla, Puṇḍravardhana, Varendri, Rāḍhā, Tāmralipta, Suhama etc. were some time or other included in the kingdom of the Pālas. Vaṅga and Gauḍa were broad divisions during this period. Puṇḍravardhana, Varendri, Rāḍhā, Tāmralipta and Suhma were parts of the Gauḍa division, while Harikela, Candradvīpa, Samataṭa and Vaṅgāla belonged to the Vaṅga division. Magadha province (now represented by the Patna and Gayā districts) was also part of Gauḍa-Vaṅga during this period.

The chronology of the Pālas is supplied by the Sārnāth inscription.[16]

The date of Mahipāla I, a ruler of the Pālas was fixed AD 1026 in this inscription. It is possible to fix the approximate dates of the predecessors and successors of Mahipāla I by counting backwards and forwards from this fixed date, i.e., AD 1026.

The Genealogy of the Pāla Kings

NAME OF THE KING	*APPROXIMATE REIGN PERIOD (IN YRS.)*	*APPROXIMATE YEAR OF ACCESSION*
Gopāla I	—	AD 750
Dharmapāla	32	AD 770
Devapāla	39	AD 810
Surapāla I	3	AD 850
Vigrahapāla I	3 (months)	AD 856
Nārāyaṇapāla	54	AD 856
Rājyapāla	32	AD 910
Gopāla II	17	AD 942
Vigrahapāla II	26	AD 960
Mahipāla I	48	AD 988
Nayapāla	15	AD 1038
Vigrahapāla III	17	AD 1054
Mahipāla II	—	AD 1072
Surapāla II	—	AD 1075
Rāmapāla	53	AD 1077
Kumārapāla	—	AD 1130
Gopāla III	—	AD 1140
Madanapāla	18	AD 1144
Govindapāla	4	AD 1158

Bhaumakaras of Orissa

The origin of the Bhaumakara dynasty in Orissa who ruled for about 150 years is still a matter of controversy. The controversy is about the original home of the Bhaumakaras and about their caste. There exist two schools of thought about this matter. B. Mishra,[17] H. Mahtab,[18] R.C. Majumdar,[19] and N.K. Sahu[20] opine that the Bhaumakaras belonged to Orissa itself, whereas R.D. Banerji,[21] R.P. Chanda,[22] K.L. Barua,[23] K.C. Panigrahi,[24] P.C. Chaudhury[25] hold the opinion that they belonged to Assam, who in course of time migrated to Orissa. *Kaliṅga-mahiṣa-mahendra bhauman guhā bhokṣanti*,[26] a passage in the *Viṣṇupurāṇa* means *guha* protected the Kaliṅgas, Mahiṣyas and Mahendra Bhaumas. According to R.C. Majumdar and B. Mishra, the expression *mahendra bhauma*s implies that the Bhauma were inhabiting the Mahendra region of the Eastern Ghāṭs. Mishra interpreted the word *mahendra-bhauma* as the Bhauma tribe of the Mahendra mountain region and suggested that the Bhuyāns were representatives of the Mahendrabhauma of the *Viṣṇu Purāṇa*.

From the copper-plate grants of the dynasty of the Bhaumakaras it is known that they had their capital at Guhadevapāṭaka or Guheśvarapāṭaka.[27]

Literally, the word *bhauma* means one who sprang from the *bhūmi* or earth. An interesting tradition recorded in the *Kalikā Purāṇa* has it that the union of Lord Viṣṇu in his Boar Incarnation and goddess Earth gave birth to a son named Naraka, who was also known as Bhauma for his being born of the *bhūmi* or earth.[28] Having come of age, Naraka went to Prāgjyotiṣapura, identified with Kāmarūpa of Assam and became the king of that place after defeating its ruler.[29] The earlier dynasties of Kāmarūpa traced their descent from Naraka.

R.D. Banerji is of the opinion that the Bhaumakaras of Orissa most probably claimed their descent from Naraka, as the kings of Kāmarūpa did.[30] He has deduced this fact from a verse *bhaumānvayādnvad-vāptajanmā*, mentioned in the Neulpur plate, which means "one who had obtained birth in the race of Bhauma (Naraka)".[31]

In the Paśupati Temple Inscription of Nepal[32] its donor Rājyamati, the daughter of Harṣavarman and the queen of Jayadeva II of Nepal, has been described as *bhagadattarājakulaja* meaning that she was the daughter of the Bhagadatta ruling family of Assam. This inscription has given credit to Harṣadeva or Harṣavarman as the conqueror of Gauḍa, Oḍra, Kaliṅga and Kosala.[33] It appears that Harṣavarman of Assam, after conquering these territories might have left some of his lieutenants in these areas. It might be possible that the leiutenant, left in charge of the Oḍra country succeeded in carving out a small principality which formed the nucleus of the Bhaumakara Kingdom in Orissa.

The fact that the Bhaumakaras of Orissa were a branch of the Bhauma family of Kāmarūpa is corroborated by the *Caurāsī* plate of Śivakaradeva which mentions the donor as a descendant of the Utkala Kula of the Bhaumas.[34] It thus appears that the Bhaumakaras belonged to the Utkala branch of the Bhauma family of Kāmarūpa, which came to Orissa in the wake of Harṣavarman's conquest.

However, B. Mishra held that the Bhaumakaras of Orissa had no connection with the Bhaumas of Assam.[35] He says that the early members of the Bhaumakara dynasty of Orissa were Buddhists, whereas all the members of the Bhauma dynasty of Assam were Śaivites. It is most probable that the early kings of the Bhaumakara dynasty gave up their ancestral faith of Śaivism and adopted Buddhism, which was the predominant religion in Orissa at that time, in order to be acceptable to the majority of the people of Orissa. That the Bhaumakaras did not completely discard their ancestral religion of Śaivism is evident not only from their construction of Śaiva shrines and their liberal donation to Śaiva ascetics, but also from the bull symbol on their seals. Thus the view of B. Mishra seems to be unconvincing to us.

From the above discussions we can assume that Kṣemaṅkara, the first king of the Bhaumakara dynasty, who laid the foundation of the Bhauma rule in Orissa, ruled as a vassal of Harṣavarman, also known as Śrī Harṣa, the King of Assam. It is just possible that after the death of Harṣavarman, the succeeding rulers of the Bhaumakara dynasty in Orissa might have thrown off the Assamese Yoke and became paramount sovereign.

According to Tāranātha,[36] Luipa, the head of a line of *tāntrika* teachers, initiated Dārika, the King of Oḍivisā (Orissa), into *tāntrika* rites. The King of Oḍivisā, referred by Tāranātha may be identified with one of the early Bhaumakara rulers of Orissa. Most probably it was King Kṣemaṅkara, who changed his religion at this time.

In the field of art and architecture both Assam and Orissa had exchanged ideas. K.C. Panigrahi refers to two images of Gaṅga, one found at Dāh Parvatiā in the Tezpur district of Assam and the other of Ratnagiri in the Cuttack district of Orissa and points out that these two images possess close resemblance stylistically and iconographically.[37] He further mentions that the Assamese specimen is earlier than the Orissan one by about three centuries, but yet the continuity of the tradition has been remarkably preserved in the latter.[38] Thus we have evidence of cultural and political connections between Assam and Orissa from very early times.

All these evidences lead us to believe that the Bhaumakaras of Orissa hailed from Assam.

The earlier copper-plate charters of the Bhaumakara dynasty refer to their family name as Bhauma while in the latter ones their family name appears as *kara*.[39] It is also seen from the genealogical table that the names of all the male rulers of this dynasty end with *kara*. The records of this dynasty represent Bhauma of the mythical fame as the progenitor of the dynasty. Hence this ruling family has been consensuously given the 'Bhauma-Kara'.

CHRONOLOGY

Another perplexing problem is the determination of the chronology of the Bhaumakara kings. The known dates of the Bhauma monarchs extend from the *saṁvat* 54 to *saṁvat* 204 without any gap, which clearly indicates that the members of this family ruled in an unbroken line of continuity for a period of atleast 150 years. The Bhaumas came to power in Orissa immediately after the fall of the Śailodbhavas. And again after the decline of the Bhaumakaras, Orissa came under the supremacy of the Somavaṁśīs. But unfortunately we find no direct reference about the Bhaumakaras period of rule in the records of the Śailodbhavas and Somavaṁśīs.

We face a great problem in reading the palaeography of the Bhaumakara inscriptions because of the use of different scripts in their inscriptions. While editing a Ganjam plate of Daṇḍi Mahādevī, F. Keilhorn pointed out that the inscription could hardly be older than thirteenth century AD[40] whereas D.C. Sircar pointed out that it belonged to tenth century AD.[41] The Bhauma rulers did not associate the name of their dynasty nor any ruler with the era, which is found in their records. Pandit B. Mishra[42] and F. Keilhorn[43] opine that the era mentioned in the Bhauma records was the Harṣa era. While H. Mahtab,[44] S.N. Rajguru,[45] K.C. Panigrahi[46] and D.C. Sircar[47] said that it was tha Bhauma era. As we get no definite clue about the Bhauma era in the Bhauma records, we have to take the help of the records of the feudatories of the Bhaumas. In the solution of our problem, the Dasapallā copper-plate grant of Ranaka Satrubhañjadeva of the Bhañja dynasty,[48] is very helpful. The Dasapallā grant, dated in the year 198,[49] was issued on the day of *visuva saṁkrānti, pañcamī, ravidina, mṛgasira nakṣatra.*[50] This grant contains such astronomical combinations as are not found frequently. The combination of the solar and lunar reckoning is rare in the Indian Calender. S.N. Rajguru,[51] while editing the Daspallā charter, consulted the 'Indian Ephemeris' of Swami Kannupillai. He has supplied the information that between the years AD 700 and AD 1100, the above astronomical combination, i.e., *visuva saṁkrānti* + *pañcamī* + *ravidina* (Sunday) occurred only thrice. The dates were (i) 21.3.812, (ii) 23.3.934, (iii) 23.3.1029. We have to fix up one of these three dates equivalent to one hundred and ninetyeighth year of the Bhauma *saṁvat*. Thus the Bhauma era should have commenced in one of the years as known here (i) AD 812 – 198 = AD 614, (ii) AD 934 – 198 = AD 736 and (iii) AD 1029 – 198 = AD 831. B. Mishra,[52] S.N. Rajguru,[53] and D.C. Sircar[54] thought that it took place respectively in the seventh, eighth and ninth centuries of the Christian era.

S.N. Rajguru has taken the 23 March, AD 934 as the date of the issue of the Dasapallā grant of Śatrubhañjadeva. He concludes that the Bhauma era started from AD 736 (934 – 198 = 736). The year AD 736 as the date of the commencement of the Bhaumakara era has also been accepted by scholars like K.C. Panigrahi[55] and N.K. Sahu.[56] This date is accepted by most of the scholars, as it does not conflict with other known dates and facts of Orissan history.

A clear chronology of the entire dynasty of the Bhaumakaras cannot be worked out as the inscriptions of several rulers of this dynasty bear no date at all. The duration of the reign period of each ruler is also difficult to determine because the Bhauma rulers have not mentioned their regnal years in their records. There were eighteen rulers including six female rulers in the Bhauma family, but their exact relationship with one another and their order of succession are not always clear. Some charters mention only the surnames of kings and maintain complete silence over their real names, which make us confused. Another difficulty is that very often the same name was borne by a number of kings and several alternate names borne by the same king. In spite of all these difficulties the genealogy of the Bhaumakaras has been reconstructed on the basis of the available dates. The list of the rulers in a chronological order with the known dates of reign is provided in the following pages.

Extent of the Bhauma Empire

As we have seen earlier that in the first half of the eighth century AD, the Bhaumakara kings of Orissa rose into eminence and held the reign of the empire up to the middle of the tenth century AD. Śivakaradeva I, the second ruler of this dynasty extended the Bhauma Kingdom for the first time and subsequently the Kingdom of the Bhaumas was extended further making it a vast one. We now discuss about the extent of the Bhauma Kingdom at its height on the basis of the land grants and other sources.

All the records of the Bhaumakaras mention the name of their kingdom as Tosāla or Tosāli. The Bhauma kingdom has been referred to as Oḍraka or Uḍra and Utkala in the records of contemporary rulers. The Sanjan plates of Amoghavarṣa, a Rāṣṭrakūṭa inscription[57] and the Brāhmeśvara temple inscription, a Somavaṁśī inscription[58] mention the Bhauma Kingdom as Oḍraka and Uḍra respectively. The Bādāl pillar inscription[59] of the time of Nārāyaṇapāla of Bengal and the Bhāgalpur plate[60] of Nārāyaṇapāla mention it as Utkala. Even the *Caurāsī* plate of Śivakara II, a Bhaumạ monarch, mention its Kingdom as Utkala.[61] We now discuss in brief about the extent of these three kingdoms.

Tosāli or Tosāla

It was divided into two large administrative units viz. *Uttara* (northern) and *Dakṣiṇa* (southern) Tosāli. According to D.C. Sircar,[62] Northen and Southern Tosāli, mentioned in the Bhauma records, roughly included modern Bālāsore, Cuttack, Purī and Ganjam districts of Orissa. But it seems that Tosāli Kingdom is much wider in extent and comprised not only the above four districts but also the modern Midnāpore, Mayūrbhañj, Keonjhar, Dhenkanāl and Baud-Phulbani districts.

Oḍra

The present Orissa derives its name from Oḍrạ of ancient times. B.C. Majumdar[63] opines, "The Hilly country lying between Kaliṅga nad Dakṣiṇa Kosala was the Oḍra land". According to H. Mahtab[64] Oḍra comprised the western Midnāpore, Eastern Singhbhūm and southern Bankura. It is generally accepted that the Oḍra or Uḍra or Wuchā comprised the whole of Midnāpore, Bālāsore and Cuttack districts as well as the northern part of Purī district.

It is interesting to see that the Bhaumakaras who ruled over the entire coastal territory from Midnāpore district to Gañjam district never called their kingdom as Oḍra, whereas some contemporary rulers refer to the said kingdom as Oḍra.

Utkala

The Bhauma king Śubhakara I styled 'the paramount Lord of Utkala, or Utkalendra in the *Caurāsī* plate of Śivakara II.[65] The contemporary Pāla records mention the Bhauma kingdom as Utkala. When the Bhauma kingdom disintegrated and the Somavaṁśīs came to power, the Somavaṁśīs records referrred the Kingdom of the Bhaumakaras as Utkala. According to S. Levi,[66] Oḍra was another name of Utkala. We may assume that Oḍra and Utkala stand for the name of the same country.[67]

Thus these three names namely Oḍra, Utkala and Tosāla or Tosāli were used as interchangeable names and each of them stood for the whole of Bhauma kingdom. The informations that we gather from different Arabian and Persian geographers also enable us to form a concrete idea about the area of Bhauma supremacy. These works mention[68] the main divisions of the Kingdom as N. Myas (Midnāpore, now in West Bengal), Harkand (Jhārakhaṇḍa, the hilly regions). Urshin (Orissa proper), K.nya (Gaṅjam), and Andras (Southern Orissa).

Thus the Bhabumakara empire, in its prime days, roughly included the territories now comprising the Midnāpore district in the north, Mayūrbhaṅja, Keonjhar, Dhenkanāl, and Baud-Phulbani districts in the West, Gaṅjam district in the south and the districts of Purī, Cuttack and Bālāsore in the east. The Bhauma kingdom, was almost of the same extent as the modern Orissa, except the Midnāpore district of West Bengal.

Capital

The place of issue of the copper-plate grants, mentioned in the records of the Bhauma rulers was in most cases Gahadevapāṭaka or Guheśvarapāṭaka. The identification of this place is a matter of controversy. S.N. Rajguru[69] is of the opinion that Khaṇḍagiri was identical with Guheśvarapāṭaka. Another scholar B. Mishra[70] has identified it with Godhaneśvarapāṭanā near Jājpur. K.C. Panigrahi[71] identifies this place with Guhirā Tikrā, five miles away from Jājpur while N.K. Sahu[72] identifies it with the present town of Jājpur. The view of N.K. Sahu is also supported by R.C. Majumdar.[73]

The Gaṅjam grant of Jayavarmadeva of Svetaka[74] reveals that the Virajā or Jājpur was the capital city of the Bhaumakaras. Virajā finds mention in the *Caurāsi* plate of Śivakaradeva II,[75] as well as, in the Dhauli inscription of the time of Śāntikaradeva I,[76] two Bhauma rulers.

Thus it may be accepted that Virajā or modern Jājpur in the district of Cuttack in Orissa was the capital of the Bhaumas as it served as the capital in the successive ruling families of the Somavaṁśīs and the Gaṅgas.

The Ganealogy of the Bhaumakara rulers

NAME OF THE RULER	*APPROX. REIGN PERIOD (IN YRS.)*	*APPROX. YEAR OF ACCESSION*
Kṣemaṅkaradeva		
Śivakaradeva I *alias* Unmattasiṁha	34	AD 756 or 786
Śubhakaradeva I	19	AD 790
Śivakaradeva II	20	AD 809
Śāntikaradeva I	7	AD 829
Śubhakaradeva II	3	AD 836
Śubhakaradeva III	7	AD 839
Tribhuvana Mahādevī I	—	AD 846
Śāntikaradeva II *alias* Gayaḍa II	—	—
Śubhakaradeva IV *alias* Kusumahāra II	8 or 4	AD 877 or 881
Sivakaradeva III *alias* Lalitahāra II	9	AD 885
Pṛthvī Mahādevi *alias* Tribhuvana Mahādevī II	—	AD 894
Śāntikaradeva III	—	—
Śubhakaradeva V	—	—
Gaurī Mahādevī	—	—
Daṇḍi Mahādevī	24 or 17	AD 916 and 923
Vakula Mahādevī	—	AD 940
Dharma Mahādevī	5	—

Notes

1. Hudud al-Alam, *The religions of the world, A Persian Geography*, translated in English, Oxford University Press, 1937, pp. 241-42.
2. *Ibid.*, p. 168.

3. Khālimpur cp, Pāla Inscriptions, *EI*, IV, 243.
4. R.C. Majumdar (ed.), *The History of Bengal*, Vol. I, p. 97.
5. *Ibid.*
6. *Ibid.*
7. *Ibid.*
8. H.P. Sastri (ed.), *Rāmcarita of Sandhyākar Nandi*, p.vi.
9. *JASB*, 1898, p. 20.
10. H.P. Sastri (ed.), *op. cit.*, p. ix.
11. R.C. Majumdar (ed.), *op. cit.*, p. 100.
12. H.P. Sastri (ed.), *op. cit.*, p. 17.
13. R.C. Majumdar (ed.), *op. cit.*, p. 101.
14. H.P. Sastri (ed.), *op. cit*.
15. R.C. Majumdar (ed.) *op. cit.*, p. 102.
16. *IA*, XIV, p. 139.
17. B. Mishra, *Orissa under the Bhauma Kings*, pp. 80-83.
18. H. Mahtab, *History of Orissa*, Vol. I, pp. 131-32.
19. R.C. Majumdar (ed.), *Age of Imperial Kanauj*, p. 63.
20. N.K. Sahu, *History of Orissa*, Vol. I, p. viii.
21. *EI*, Vol. XV, pp. 1-8.
22. *Paravāsi*, Vol. XXXII, AO.1.
23. *JARS*, Vol. II, p. 106.
24. K.C. Panigrahi, *Chronology of the Bhauma-Karas and Somavamsis of Orissa*, p. 21.
25. P.C. Chowdhury, *History of Civilization of the people of Assam*, p. 198.
26. H.H. Wilson (tr.), *Viṣṇu Purāṇa*, IV, (1865), p. 220.
27. B. Mishra, *op. cit.*, p. 87.
28. *JARS*, X, 1 and 2 (1943), p. 14.
29. K.L. Barua, *Early History of Kāmarūpa*, (1933), p. 1.
30. *EI*, XV, (1919-20), p. 2.
31. *Ibid.*, p. 5.
32. *IA*, IX, (1980) pp. 178-83.
33. *Ibid.*, p. 181.
34. *JBORS*, XIV, ii, 1928, pp. 292-306.

35. B. Mishra, *op. cit.* (1934) p. 83.
36. R.C. Majumdar (ed.), *Age of Imperial Kanauj*, p. 268.
37. K.C. Panigrahi, *Chronology of the Bhauma-Karas and Somavamsis of Orissa*, pp. 21-22.
38. *Ibid.*, p. 22.
39. B. Mishra, *op. cit.*, p. 13.
40. *EI*, Vol. VI, p. 136.
41. *PIHC*, 1949, p. 128.
42. B. Mishra, *op. cit.*, p. 72.
43. *SII*, Vol. II, p. 508.
44. H. Mahtab, *History of Orissa*, Vol. I, p. 130.
45. *OHRJ*, Vol. XII, pp. 100 ff.
46. K.C. Panigrahi, *op. cit.*, pp. 8-9.
47. *EI*, Vol. XXIX, p. 189.
48. *OHRJ*, I (iii) (October, 1952) pp. 208-13.
49. *Ibid.*, p. 208.
50. *Ibid.*, p. 209.
51. *Ibid.*
52. B. Mishra, *op. cit.*, pp. 72 ff.
53. *OHRJ*, Vol. V, pp. 68 ff.
54. *EI*, Vol. XXI, pp. 189 ff.
55. Panigrahi, *op cit.*, p. 18.
56. Sahu (ed.), *op. cit.*, p. 347.
57. R.C. Majumdar (ed.), *Age of Imperial Kanauj*, p. 7.
58. *JASB* (Letter), Vol. XIII, p. 72.
59. *EI*, Vol. II, p. 165.
60. *IA*, Vol. XV, pp. 304 ff.
61. *JBORS*, Vol. XIV, pp. 292 ff.
62. *EI*, XXXX, (1951-52) p. 85.
63. R.C. Majumdar, *Orissa in the making*, p. 16.
64. H. Mahtab, *History of Orissa*, Vol. I, p. 2.
65. *JBORS*, Vol. XIV, pp. 292-306.
66. P. Bagchi, *Pre-Aryan and Pre-Dravidians in India*, p. 84.

67. *OHRJ*, Vol. I, p. 91.
68. K.C. Panigrahi, *History of Orissa*, p. 91.
69. *JAHRS*, Vol. IV, p. 192.
70. B. Mishra, *Orissa under the Bhauma Kings*, p. 89.
71. K.C. Panigarhi, *Chronology of the Bhaumakaras and Somavamsis of Orissa*, p. 22.
72. N.K. Sahu, *History of Orissa* I, p. 109.
73. R.C. Majumdar (ed.), *Age of Imperial Kanauj*, p. 69.
74. *IHQ*, Vol. XII, pp. 189-91.
75. B. Mishra, *op. cit.*, p. 8.
76. *EI*, Vol. XIX (1927-28), pp. 263-64.

2

Position of Buddhism in Bengal and Orissa Prior to the Eighth Century AD

BENGAL

BENGAL of our period consisted of the present West Bengal, Bangladesh and the province of Magadha in Bihar. Two main geographical divisions called Gauḍa and Vaṅga were under the Pālas of Bengal. Gauḍa had many sub-divisions like Puṇḍṛavardhana, Varendri, Rāḍhā, Tāmralipta and Suhma and similarly Vaṅga had Harikela, Candradvīpa, Samataṭa and Vaṅgāla.

It is very difficult to say when Buddhism first gained influence in Bengal. In a passage of *Vinaya* text written in Sanskrit, the eastern limit of ordination is stated to be the kingdom of Puṇḍravardhana. From this statement it is assumed that Buddhism probably had obtained a footing in North Bengal even before Aśoka's time. No authentic Buddhist source give any positive evidence that Buddhism was current in Bengal during the lifetime of Buddha. But later texts like the *Travels of Yaun Chwang* and the Tibetan Monk Sumpa's *Pag-sam-Jon-Zang* mentioned that Buddha undertook a missionary tour in Puṇḍravardhana, and his messages reached Samataṭa and Karnasuvarna. These facts are yet to be proved because till now no archaeological or literary source had corroborated this fact.

According to a tradition recorded in the *Divyāvadāna*,[1] Buddhism was flourishing along with Jainism in Puṇḍravardhana during Aśoka's period. This text mentioned Puṇḍravardhana as the eastern most boundary of the Buddhist *Madhyadeśa*. Yuan Chwang confirms this, as he refers to the erection of numerous *stūpa*s in Puṇḍravardhana and other regions of Bengal by Aśoka.[2] But unfortunately no Aśokan *stūpa* or edict of Aśoka has so far been discovered in Bengal, which is really very surprising.

The existence of Buddhism in North Bengal in the second century BC may be inferred from two votice inscriptions at Sāncī, recording the gifts of two inhabitants of Punavadhana, which undoubtedly stands for Puṇḍravardhana.[3] The first definite reference to Vaṅga, as an important centre of Buddhism occurs in the Nāgārjunakoṇḍa inscriptions, which may be dated in the second and third centuries AD.[4] It includes Vaṅga in a long list of well-known countries which were converted to Buddhism by the masters and fraternities of Ceylonese Monks. It appears that Buddhism made its entry into Bengal before the close of the pre-Christian era. The discovery of several Buddhist images of third-fourth century AD at Chandraketugarh (24-Pargana in West Bengal) was a concrete proof of the existence of Buddhism in an established form by the beginning of the fifth century AD.[5]

Bengal was under the Guptas for quite a substantial period of time. During the rule of Śrī Gupta, Buddhism got the royal patronage in Bengal. It is learnt from the accounts of I-tsing that Mahārāja Śrī Gupta built a temple called 'Temple of China' at a place close to a sanctuary called *Mi-li-kia-si-kia-po-no*.[6] He further says[7] that the King donated twenty-four villages for the maintenance of the temple and a building was constructed for the accommodation of foreign scholars particularly Chinese visitors, as the name suggests. The site of the 'Temple of China' has been located at Māldāh.[8]

Fa-hien, another Chinese Pilgrim who came to India in the beginning of fifth century AD, saw Buddhism in a flourishing condition at Tāmralipti (Tāmluk in Midnāpore district of West Bengal). He described that in

Tāmralipti, there were twenty-two monasteries, all of which were inhabitated by monks and he himself stayed there for two years when he wrote out his *Sūtras* and drew pictures of images.[9] It is learnt from Gupta King Vainyagupta's Gunaighar copper-plate grant of 188 Gupta Era (AD 507-8) that he donated the land on the request of his officer in order to meet the expenses for worshipping Buddha in the monastery of Avalokiteśvara which was built in honour of Ācarya Śāntideva.[10] This example shows that Buddhisn had been firmly established even in the remote south-eastern corner of Bengal by the beginning of the sixth century AD. The discovery of a few Buddhist sculptures from Rājaśāhī belonging to the Gupta period proves beyond doubt the firm existence of Buddhism in Bengal during the Gupta period.

A number of Chinese records of the seventh century contained information on the condition of Buddhism in Bengal. Among all these records the accounts of Hiuen-Tsang, is of course, noteworthy. He saw while his stay in India almost all important Buddhist centres in Bengal. At Kajangala[11] near Rājmahal he saw six or seven Buddhist monasteries which contained over three hundred brethren. At Puṇḍravardhana[12] there were twenty Buddhist monasteries and above 3000 brethern, who followed the *Mahāyāna* and *Hīnayāna* schools of Buddhist philosophy. The biggest establishment at Puṇḍravardhana was *Po-shi-po* monastery,[13] which had spacious halls and tall storyed chambers and had over seven hundred brethren and many distinguished monks of Eastern India. In Samataṭa there were more than thirty Buddhist monasteries with above 2000 brethren of the *Sthavira* School, in Karnasuvarna, more than ten monasteries with above 2000 brethren of the *Sammatīya* school and in Tāmralipti more than ten monasteries with above 1000 brethren.[14] Huen-Tsang also saw a monastery *Lo-to-mo-chi* at Karnasuvarna which was a resort of illustrious brethren.[15]

Another Chinese pilgrim in India was Ta-cheng-teng. He described about the condition of Buddhism in Tāmralipti as he stayed at Tāmralipti for twelve years and acquired extensive knowledge about various Sanskrit Buddhist texts. Another Chinese Tao-lin came to Tāmralipti and stayed there for three years to learn Sanskrit. While staying there he got himself initiated to the *Sarvāstivāda* school.[16]

Sheng-chi, who was in India about seventh century AD has recorded a valuable piece of evidence on the condition of Buddhism is Samataṭa.[17] Rājabhaṭa, the king of Samataṭa was a fervent worshipper of Tri-ratna and played the part of a great *upāsaka*. He used to make, everyday, hundred thousand statues of Buddha with earth which seems impossible and read hundred thousand *ślokas* of the *Mahāprajñāpāramitā-sūtra*. He also used to take out processions in honour of Buddha, with an image of Avalokiteśvara at the front, and make pious gifts. In that city there were more than four thousand monks and nuns. Though some informations provided by Sheng-chi seem practically impossible, still his description proves beyond doubt the flourishing condition of Buddhism in Samataṭa region of Bengal in the seventh century AD.

Śaśāṅka, the ruler of Gauḍa in the early seventh century has been charged with persecution of Buddhists by Bānabhaṭṭa and Hiuen Tsang. As we have no concrete evidence of Śaśāṅka's anti-Buddhist activities, a correct estimate of him, has not been possible. Śaśāṅka's devotion to Śaivism does not necessarily prove his hostility towards Buddhism. As our knowledge about Śaśāṅka's anti-Buddhist activities is gathered from the writings of Buddhists, it is very difficult to determine how far Śaśāṅka was against Buddhism.

Buddhism was confined to Vaṅga-Samataṭa region of Bengal at the time of the death of Śaśāṅka (around AD 637). The second half of the seventh century AD saw a number of Buddhist kings with Khaḍgas as a part of their names in Vaṅga-Samataṭa region. The knowledge about this dynasty was provided by the discovery of two copper-plates at Ashrafpur[18] (30 miles north-east of Dacca) and an inscribed image of *Sarvāṇī* discovered at Deulbad.[19] (near Comilla in Bangladesh). The Ashrafpur copper-plate characters were issued at the behest of Devakhaḍga and in the opening verse of the two plates the name Buddha has been invoked. In another verse Khaḍgodyama has been credited with military successes after he had shown devotion towards Sugata (Buddha), His *Dharma* and His *Saṅgha*. The donee of both of these plates was Sanghamitra, a famous Buddhist teacher. The informations gained from these two Ashrafpur plates confirm that the Khaḍgas of Vaṅga-Samataṭa were devout Buddhists and did their best for the furtherance of their religious faith.

A copper-plate discovered at Kailan,[20] near Comilla in Bangladesh was issued by Śrīdharāna-Rāta a semi-feudatory ruler, who was a *Parama Vaiṣṇava*. It states that Śrīdharāna's chief minister of peace and war Jayanātha prayed him for twenty-five *pātakas* of land for the purpose of dividing the granted land between two different religious worshipful objects, which included the provision for the garlands, light, incence etc. for Lord Tathāgata (Buddha) for the study and recitation of the *Dharma* and for the provision of various requisites like robes and food-lumps for the noble *Saṅgha*. He also wanted to make a distribution of certain portion of the granted land to some learned brāhmaṇas. The request was granted by the ruler which showed the religious chatholicity of that age.

The discovery of three copper-plates issued by Bhavadeva Salban Vihara of the Maināmati region in Comilla district of Bangladesh, unveiled the history of a Buddhist dynasty called the Devas.[21] This family had four ruling members who bore the epithets like Paramasaugata, Paramabhaṭṭāraka etc. This ruling family like Khaḍgas and Rāṭas, also professed and propagated Buddhism, as is evident from the plates bearing the Buddhist *Dharmacakra-deer* symbol.

It is very significant to notice that not a single grant made exclusively in favour of a brāhmaṇa cult has yet been discovered from the Vaṅga-Samataṭa region over which the Khaḍgas, the Rāṭas and the Devas ruled in the seventh-eighth century AD.[22]

As regards the schools of Buddhism prevailing in Bengal before the advent of the Pālas, Hiuen Tsang[23] tells us that in Puṇḍravardhana there were both *Hīnayāna* and *Mahāyāna*, Karnasuvarna the *Sammatīya* school (a branch of *Sarvāstivāda*), in Tāmralipti the *Sarvāstivāda* and in Samataṭa the *Mahāyāna*.

I-tsing[24] tells us that all the four schools viz. the *Mahāsāṅghika*, *Sthaviravāda*, *Sarvāstivāda* and *Sammatīya* were prevalent in Eastern India. It seems that the difference between *Hīnayāna* and *Mahāyāna* did not present itself to the Buddhist monks of those days in the same way as it does now.

As a matter of fact the religious life in India is marked about this time by a spirit of catholicity and mutual respect and understanding. The differnences between the religious sects were fast coming down. The ruler, the religious leaders and the people played a significant role in the maintenance of such a spirit of tolerance and mutual respect among different religious sects.

ORISSA

Ancient scriptures have rightly attested Orissa as a busy place of religious culture. This land shows a wonderful spirit of assimilation of various religious faiths in its breast from the Vedic belief to the unorthodox faith of Buddhism.

The history of Buddhism in Orissa prior to the Aśokan period is not yet clear to us because of the absence of authentic source materials. Though Kaliṅga (the ancient name of Orissa) found emphatic expression in the different Buddhist texts including the *Jātaka*s, it is quite difficult to determine at what particular period of time, Buddhism entered into Orissa. The early Buddhist texts, recording the life and travels of the Buddha, do not mention anything about the personal visit of Buddha to Kaliṅga. However, the Chinese records[25] mention that Buddha had a high regard for the spiritual heritage of Kaliṅga which he declared as one of the twelve places where the attainment of perfection might be sought.

Tapassu (Tapussa) and Bhalluka (Bhallika or Bhalliya), the two merchant brothers of *Ukkala* are said to be the first lay disciples of the Buddha by the *Mahāvagga* of *Vinaya* text, the *Aṅguttara Nikāya* of *Suttapiṭaka* as well as by the *Jātakas*.[26] According to the accounts of these Pāli literature when the Blessed one was enjoying the bliss of emancipation at the foot of the Rājayātana tree in the eighth week after his Enlightenment, these two merchants are stated to have passed by his side with five hundred trading carts enroute to the middle country. The two brothers offered the Buddha rice cakes and lump of honey, as they heard a divine voice directing them to do so. These two merchants then prayed

Buddha to take them as his disciples.[27] Buddha stroked his head eight times and offered his hair to the merchants which they took to their city to enshrine in a magnificent *caitya*. Thus Tapassu and Bhallika are regarded as the first disciples of the Buddha, and their formula of Refuge, as embodied in the *Mahāvagga* of the *Vinaya* text, contained the *dyad* and not the *triad*.[28] Tapassu, in course of time, became a *sotāpanna* and as *devācika upāsaka* was included in the list of eminent *upāsaka*s, while Bhallika entered the *Saṅgha* and turned an *arhat*.[29] In Orissa's legends and folklore, the ancient merchant princes are described as cultured. It can be assumed that after their return from this memorable trip, the two merchants must have taken great interest in spreading the teachings of Buddha among their compatriots.

There is controversy over the location of Ukkala, the native place of these two merchants Tapassu and Bhallika. The *Lalitavistāra* and the *Mahāvastu* place Ukkala in the north-west of India. As these texts were of later origin, it is difficult to believe this identification. The Burmese records claimed that these two merchant tribes were the inhabitants of the city of Okkalaba of the Irrawaddy valley in Burma (now Myanmar), which is not believed by the scholars. Majority of the scholars believe that the name Ukkala of the Pāli texts is the present Orissa.

Another source of our information about the existence of Buddhism in Orissa in the ancient age is the *Daṭhavaṁsa*, a quasi religio-political record of Sri Lanka. While mentioning about the distribution of the sacred relic of the Buddha, it states that a tooth relic was taken by Khema to the court of Brahmadatta, the king of Kaliṅga, who built a magnificent *caitya* over it in his capital Dantapura.[30] As the *Mahāparinibbāna Sutta* of the *Dīgha Nikāya* did not mention about the name of Kaliṅga in the list of the countries to which Buddha's body relic was taken, it is difficult to believe the facts given by *Daṭhavaṁsa*, a text of the later period.

The existence of Buddhism in Orissa prior to Aśoka's reign was evident from his Rock Edict XIII, which mentions that among the large number of people who suffered in the devastating Kaliṅga War were brāhmaṇas, śramaṇas and others. The term sramaṇas is meant for the followers of Buddhism. So Buddhism was not unknown to Orissa before the Kaliṅga

War.

One of the greatest landmarks in the history of Buddhism was the Kaliṅga War. The destruction and the loss of lives in this War made Aśoka so remorse that he said good bye to war and was converted to Buddhism as its simplicity and concept of non-violence impressed him very much. As a result of Kaliṅga's inclusion in the empire of Aśoka, Buddhism received a new spirit and vigour. Tissā, the brother of Aśoka chose Kaliṅga to be the place of his retirement and the emperor built there for him a monastery known as the Bhojakgiri *vihāra*, which became the centre of activities of the **Thera school.**[31] Aśoka undertook various constructive works in Orissa in order to enhance the status of Buddhism, the remnants of which are found even today. His edicts of Dhaulī near Bhubanesvar and Jaugarh in the Gaṅjam district of Orissa were intended to attract people towards Buddhism. In both these Rock Edict inscriptions the Edicts XI, XII and XIII are lacking. They are arranged in three distinct columns, the middle column containing the Edicts I to IV and the right column consisting of the Edicts VII to X and XIV. Below the right column is engraved the second separate Edict bordered by straight lines, while the whole of the left column is devoted to the first separate Edict. Both Dhaulī and Jaugarh areas are sorrounded by the debris of antiquities which were certainly important centres of Buddhist activities during the Aśokan reign. Yuan Chwang mentioned about this when he wrote that Aśoka built more than ten *stūpas* in Wu-t'u (Oḍra or Orissa).[32] R.L. Mitra could trace in the Dhaulī area immediately above the Rock Edicts a structure which he thought to be a *caitya* or *stūpa.*[33] And interesting discovery of this area is the collosal figure of the forepart of an elephant, a symbol of Buddhists about four feet in height, which is hewn out of the solid rock. The figure is very similar to the elephant figure on the Aśokan Rock Edict at Kālsi.

At Bhubanesvar, not far from Dhaulī, the presence of an Aśokan Pillar has been a subject of discussion among different scholars. The remnants of Aśokan Pillar are found in and around the temple of Bhāskareśvara temple in Bhubanesvar. The unusual large sized *liṅgam* in the Bhāskareśvara temple, doubted to be the Aśokan column, the upper portion of the lion and a railing pillar dug out from the area near this temple, and the discovery of the portion of the capital consisting of the abacus, the torus and the bell from the Aśoka Jhara tank near the Rāmeśvara temple, not far from Bhāskareśvara temple are the reasons behind the assumption that there was a Aśokan Pillar in Bhubanesvar. Scholars like M.L. Mitra, M.M. Ganguli, N.K. Bose and K.C. Panigrahi are unanimous about the presence of as Aśokan Pillar at Bhubanesvar.

Another controversy is about the presence of a *stūpa* in Bhubnesvar. The discovery of the corner post of a railing near the Bhāskareśvara temple by Prof. R.K. Mukherji in 1926 and subsequently the discovery of broken posts near the Bhāskaraeśvara temple gave rise to the suggestion that the site of an ancient *stūpa* must be existing somewhere near about the spot. Like the other railing posts at the *stūpa*s of Bhārhut, Bodh Gayā and Sāncī, this one has also four sides with pictures of human figures carved in bold relief. This railing has been assigned to the period of first century BC, contemporary with the Sāncī *stūpa*.[34]

The discovery of four *Yakṣa* statues near Khaṇḍagiri in Bhubanesvar which are now preserved in the Orissa Museum, further confirms the existence of a *stūpa* in Bhubanesvar. The statues are strikingly similar to those of the *Yakṣa*s forming the capitals of the pillars in the gateway of Sāncī. Thus it is reasonable to believe that there existed a *stūpa* at Bhubanesvar, contemporary with the great *stūpa* of Sāncī.

After the Aśokan age, there is no archaeological evidence of the Buddhistic activities till the post-Gupta period. This great gap appears very strange when we think of the religious activities of the people of Orissa during the very ancient age. It is very difficult to give any reason for this unless we presume that the artistic products of this age were all made of perishable materials or they are not yet been discovered.

We get information about the condition of Buddhism in Orissa in the post-Gupta period from the accounts given by the Chinese pilgrim Hiuen-Tsang. Hiuen-Tsang mentioned about *Puṣpagiri* (*peu-su-po-ki-li*) monastery, which he considered to be one of the most wonderful monasteries of the Buddhist world. He was so impressed by the miraculous powers of its *stūpa*s and *caitya*s that he thought them to have been built not by human hands but by demons.[35] The location of this famous religious centre remains unfortunately a disputed problem. Yuan Chwang locates it in the south-west frontier of Wu-tu country. Thus it may be located to the south-west of Jājpur, i.e., Lalitagiri, Udayagiri and Ratnagiri area.[36]

Huen Tsang states that in the Oḍra country (North Orissa) there were some hundred *Saṅghārāmas* (monasteries) with 10,000 monks, all of whom were followers of the *Mahāyāna* Buddhism.[37] He found Buddhism in thriving condition in the south Kosala region of Orissa also. He mentions[38] that the king of this region was a kṣatriya, but he greatly honoured the Law of the Buddha. There were about one hundred monasteries with less than ten thousand monks. Just outside this country famous there was an old (Buddhist) monastery and a *stūpa*, built by Aśoka. The Nāgārjuna was at one time a resident of this monastery.

Though Oḍra and south Kosala were important centres of Buddhism during the seventh century AD, in other areas of Orissa Buddhism was in a declining state. Regarding Buddhism in Kongoḍa in Orissa, Hiuen Tsang mentions[39] that the people of this land did not believe in the Law of Buddha, as they greatly respected the teachings of heretics. About Kaliṅga he states[40] that there were very few Buddhists, as he found less than ten Buddhist monasteries with only five hundred monks, whereas there were many *Deva* temples.

Buddhism in Orissa was not in a flourishing state till the rise of the Bhaumakaras. This fact may be attributed to the lack of royal patronage. The Śailodbhavas, who ruled over Kongoḍa in the seventh and eighth centuries AD, were strongly pro-brāhmaṇic. It is likely that the kings of this dynasty diverted their patronage from the Buddhist monasteries to the brāhmaṇic temples and Institutions. That is why Tāranātha describes that at that time the *śrāvaka* monks dwelling in the south were dwindling in number.[41] Notable Buddhist rulers do not seem to have flourished in Orissa prior to the Bhaumakaras. Though there was no royal patronage before the eighth century AD, Buddhism is known to have thrived in Orissa due to popular support only, which is a very significant development.

Notes

1. *Divyāvadāna*, ed. by Cowell, p. 427.
2. *Yuan Chwang's Accounts*, tr. by Walters, Vol. II, p. 184-85.
3. *EI*, Vol. II, p. 108-380.
4. *EI*, Vol. XX, p. 23.
5. Indian Archaeology (9A — 1957-58, p. 72).
6. S. Beal, *Life of Hiuen Tsang*, p. xxxvi.
7. Chavannes, *Religieux Eminents*, pp. 82-83.
8. S. Chatopadhyaya, *Early History of North India*, p. 137-38.
9. J. Legge (tr.), *Fahien's Records of Buddhistic Kingdom*, p. 108.
10. *IHQ*, VI, pp. 45-60.
11. Walters (tr.), *Accounts of Huen Tsang II*, p. 182-93 and S. Beals *Records II*, p. 193-204.
12. *Ibid.*
13. *Ibid.*
14. *Ibid.*
15. *Ibid.*
16. Chavannes (tr.), *Religieux Eminents*, p. 94.
17. *Ibid.*, p. 128.
18. *MASB*, I, pp. 85-91.
19. *EI*, XVII, pp. 357 ff.
20. *IHQ*, XXIII, 1947 pp. 221-41.
21. F.A. Khan, *Maināmati*, Karachi, 1963, pp. 19ff. 3rd Plate (2 plates) ed. by D.C. Sircar in *JASB*, XVII, pp. 83 ff.
22. G.S. Majumdar, *Buddhism in Ancient Bengal*, p. 20.
23. Walters (tr.), *Accounts of Hiuen Tsang II*, p. 188-93.
24. Chavannas (tr.), *Religieux Eminents*, pp. 82-83.
25. Walters, *Yuan Chwang*, Vol. II, p. 199.
26. Pali Text Society, Vol. I, p. 213, Vol. II. pp. 252, 256, 260.
27. *OHRJ*, Vol. IV, 3 and 4, 1956, p. 81.
28. *Dyad* — taking refuse in the Buddha and in the *Dharma, Triad* — taking refuse in the Buddha, *Dharma* and *Saṅgha*, N.K. Sahu, *Buddhism in Orissa*, p.9.
29. *OHRJ*, Vol. IV, No. 3 and 4, 1956, p. 81.

30. *Ibid.*, p. 86.
31. *Ibid.*, p. 189.
32. S. Beal, *Buddhist Records of the Western World*, Delhi, p. 205.
33. R.L. Mitra, *Antiquities of Orissa*, II, p. 47.
34. N.K. Sahu, *Buddhism in Orissa*, p. 33.
35. Beal, *Buddhist Records*, II, p. 205.
36. *MASI*, No. 44, *Exploration in Orissa*, p.6.
37. Beal, *Buddhist Records*, II, p. 204.
38. *Ibid.*, p. 409-10.
39. *Ibid.*, p. 206.
40. *Ibid.*, p. 208.
41. D.P. Chattopadhyaya (tr.), *History of Buddhism in India* by Tāranāth, Calcutta., 1970, p. 201.

3

Buddhism in Bengal and Orissa

PĀLA AGE

THE glorious period of Buddhism in its history in eastern India was the period of the Pālas who ruled over Bengal and Bihar from eighth to twelfth century AD. We get an idea about the religious conditions of Bengal from the land grant inscriptions as well as other documents of the Pāla rulers. Though the Pāla rulers were staunch followers of Buddhism, they were not sectarian in their belief. In fact in persuance of the policy of their forefathers, they in a great extent supported the brāhmaṇic religion. This shows the catholic nature of the Pālas.

From the epigraphic records we come to know that the Pāla rulers call themselves *parama-saugata* and the Buddha is regularly invoked at the beginning of their official records. The Pāla kings devoted themselves wholheartedly to the service of Buddhism. They tried to spread the teachings of Buddha not only in thier sphere of influence but also in other parts of their kingdom. During the four centuries of their rule, Bengal and Bihar remained the last strong hold of Buddhism. It was due to the concerted efforts of the Pālas that Buddhism became a powerful force in the international field and exercised dominant influence from Tibet in the north to the islands of the Mālaya Archipelago in the south.

Buddhism became a strong force in Bengal under the Pāla rulers particularly under strong rulers like Dharmapāla, Devapāla, Mahipāla I, Nayapāla and Rāmapāla. The foundations of many important Buddhist monasteries like Odantapuri, Somapura, Vikramaśilā and many others were laid by the early Pāla Kings.

Tāranātha[1] states that Gopāla, the first king of the Pāla dynasty, was a great *upāsaka* and attained *siddhi* by worshipping the Goddess Cuṇḍa, a Buddhist Tāntric God, before his nomination as king of Bengal. It is quite natural that after the assumption of the throne Gopāla must have made sincere efforts for the propagation of Buddhism. According to the Tibetan tradition[2] Gopāla was credited with the establishment of the Odantapura Mahāvihāra on the model of Nālandā Mahāvihāra, which is very near to it. But it is still difficult for us to ascertain who the builder of the Odantapura Mahāvihāra was, as other scholars give the credit of building this monastery to Dharmapāla or Devapāla. From Tāranātha's long list of Buddhist scholars, who flourished during the rule of Gopāla, we can onclude that there was a brisk era of Buddhist activities during his reign.

Dharmapāla who succeeded Gopāla not only consolidated his empire, but also firmly established Buddhism in Bengal. Tibetan chronicles described in detail about the patronage of Dharmapāla to the Buddhist faith. Dharmapāla is credited with the establishment of the Vikramaśilā in Magadha. This *vihāra*, which had 107 temples and six colleges and life sized image of the Buddha, was one of the greatest works of Dharmapāla. It outshone Nālandā by attracting a large number of Buddhist students from Tibet. Tāranātha states that for studying Buddhist doctrine Dharmapāla built fifty centres in this *vihāra*. The credit of the establishment of the Vikramaśilā monastery is given to Dharmapāla on the basis of the second name of Dharmapāla which was Śrī-Vikrama-Śiladeva.[3] So also the clay seals recovered among the ruins of Paharpur in Bangladesh, reveal the name of Dharmapāla as the founder of the Somapuri Vihara in Varendra.[4] Dharmapāla provided encouragement and financial help to various scholars on Buddhism for writing Buddhist philosophical texts. Thus an era of Buddhist literary works started from this period.

Devapāla, the third ruler of the Pāla dynasty continued the unfinished work of his father and zealously involved himself for the propagation of Buddhism. His Nālandā copper-plate inscription throws light on his role as a patron of Buddhism. The discovery of a large number of Buddhist images or relics consecrated by the common people in Magadha during the period of Devapāla shows the popularity of Buddhism in Magadha and Bengal. The Monghyr copper-plate describes, "Devapāladeva as the devout worshipper of Sugata".[5] The Nālandā copper-plate of Devapāla reveals[6] that on the request of Bālaputradeva of the Sailendra dynasty of Jāvā, who built a monastery at Nālandā, King Devapāla made grants of five villages for the maintenance of the monastery. Tāranātha mentions[7] that Devapāla was the founder of the Somapuri Monastery at Varendra. But this fact has been proved to be wrong by the discovery of clay seals from Paharpur, which has been discussed above.

Due to lack of strong rulers after the death of Devapāla Bengal was distintegrated. The epigraphic records of the religious activities of the rulers of this period are very few in number and so also the Tibetan chronicles were silent on this issue. But it is difficult to believe that the Pāla rulers withdrew their support from Buddhism. It is a fact that the rulers during this period were so busy in maintaining the integrity of their kingdom that they hardly found any time to think about the religion. Indeed, they remained as devout Buddhists as their forefathers were.

Surapāla succeeded his father Devapāla and he has been described in the Mirzāpur copper-plate as *parama-saugata*.[8] Two other records[9] found somewhere in Bihar, inscribed on the pedestal of two images of Buddha, are reportedly contain the name of Uddaṇḍapura (Odantapuri) and they record that the images were installed by Pūrṇadāsa, a Buddhist monk of Sind, in the third regnal year of Surapāla. Unfortunately the reign of Surapāla was short lived as he abdicated his throne in favour of his son Nārāyaṇapāla.

Though Nārāyaṇapāla reigned for about 54 years, no evidence of his support to Buddhism has so far come to us. But from the presence of Buddhistic emblem of *dharmacakra* and invocation in his inscriptions, we are sure that Nārāyaṇapāla had deep faith and devotion to Buddhism.

From one of the inscriptions of Nārāyaṇapāla we find that a monk named Dharmamitra installed an image of Buddha in some place in Magadha during the ninth regnal year of Nārāyaṇapāla.[10]

The reign of Rājyapāla, the successor of Nārāyaṇapāla was not significant so far as Buddhism is concerned. But Rājyapāla's son and successor Gopāla II's reign was very significant from the point of view of Buddhism. The pedestal of a Buddha statue discoverd at Bodh Gayā and the inscription on it reveals the name of Sukrasena, who consecrated the Buddha image during Gopāla II's reign.[11] This example proves his devotion for Buddhism.

The rule of Vigrahapāla II was not very fruitful in the sphere of religion as he was not even capable to check the disintegration of his kingdom.

Thus the period from the death of Devapāla to the rise of Mahipāla I (from AD 850 to 988) was a period of decadence for the Pālas. Buddhism could not get the same patronage as was receiving earlier, due to the political instability. But Buddhism as a faith did not evaporate from Bengal due to the sincere devotion of the common men as is indicated by several Buddhist images bearing the names of private individuals consecrating them as a well as donating them.

After the accession of Mahipāla I, stability was established in the Pāla kingdom. Thus Buddhism got its chance to improve. The epigraphic records reveal that Mahipāla I patronised Buddhism to a great extent. The Sārnāth inscription of Mahipāla I[12] informs us that the king entrusted his two brothers for the construction of a temple of Buddha (*gandha-kuṭi*) and for the reparation of numerous Buddhist temples and *caitya*s including the shrine where Buddha preached for the first time. Likewise Nālandā stone inscription reveals that the repairs and renewals of Nālandā monastery were undertaken during his reign by Bālāditya who was a Mahāyānist.[13] In addition to this it is known from Tibetan tradition that the Somapuri monastery was in a prospering state during the reign of Mahipāla I. Another stone inscription found at Nālandā[14] reveals that the image of the Master in *bhūmisparśamudrā* was installed by *paramabhaṭṭāraka* Mahipāladeva in his eleventh regnal year. It seems from the Tibetan sources that Tāntric Buddhism flourished during this period.[15]

The next important Pāla king Nayapāla had great contributions for the cause of Buddhism. It was the period when the monasteries of Vikramaśilā in Magadha and Somapura in Bengal rose to their height of fame. Many scholars and monks from different parts of India as well from Tibet came to study in these monasteries. Buddhist scholars who had studied in these monasteries during this period included Lochab from Tibet, Ratnākara Sānti and Atiśa-Dipaṅkara. A Bengalee monk from Varendra (North Bengal) during this period (in 1026) went to China with many Sanskrit texts.[16]

It was the period when Buddhism made significant journey to Tibet, Japan and Nepal. We see that many of the Buddhist texts written in this period are now preserved in the Hō-ryū-ji Temple of Japan. So also we find many copied Buddhist manuscripts of this period in private and public collections in Nepal.

It was during this period that a large number of Indian scholars on Buddhism went to Tibet where they translated many Buddhist treaties in the language of that land, in collaboration with local scholars. Another significant development of this period was the emergence of the Varnacular literature in the *dohā*s and songs, composed by the Buddhist *siddhācārya*s. This period also saw the transformation of Buddhism into Tāntrikism as we find many *tāntrika* gods and goddesses entered into Buddhism.

The all round prosperity of Buddhism during Nayapāla's reign can be deduced from the Tibetan sources. They say[17] that some temples of Nālandā monastery were destroyed by the heretical king Karna of the West, who invaded the Kingdom of Nayapāla and due to Atiśa-Dipaṅkara's mediation, amity was restored between these two kings. This shows clearly that the contemporary non-Buddhist rulers did not like the prosperity of Buddhism in the reign of Nayapāla for which Nālandā monastery was attacked.

The sons and successors of Nayapāla were weak rulers who could not rule properly, resulting anarchy. So in this atmosphere Buddhism could not get the suitable royal patronage and thus started the declining phase of Buddhism.

The last outstanding contribution for the cause of Buddhism had come from the last significant Pāla king Rāmapāla, who was a great devotee of Buddhism. Sandhyākaranandī of *Rāmacarita* describes[18] Rāmāvatī, the capital of Rāmapāla, as containing the population of *bhikṣus* and an image of Avalokiteśvara, a Buddhist diety. This text gives the authorship of the great monastery named Jagaddala-Vihāra to Rāmapāla. An image of Tārā, installed at the ancient Uddaṇḍapura, fortress in the second regnal year of Rāmapāla, is now preserved in the Indian Museum, Calcutta.

Though Tibetan sources indicate the flourishing condition of Buddhism during Rāmapāla's reign, Tāranātha refers to the gradual increase in the number of heretics (*tirthikas*) and *mlecchas* in the kingdom of Bengal during this period.[20]

Due to inefficiency of the Pāla monarchs in the twelfth century, the vast Pāla empire gradually disintegrated. Though Buddhism could not prosper significantly, still it continued to get the royal support till the end of the Pāla rule. Some examples of the Buddhist activities in Bengal during the last phase of Pāla rule are described below. In the fifteenth regnal year of Gopāla III, a copy of the *Asṭasāhasrika-prajñāpāramitā*[21] was made in the Vikramśilā- Mahāvihāra, which is now preserved in the British Museum. The Manahali grant[22] (Dinājpur dist.) of Madanapāla, another king of the Pāla dynasty, bearing the usual *dharmacakra*-seal and beginning with *oṃ namo buddhāya*, speaks of the patronage of the king enjoyed by Buddhism during this period. Some Buddhist images with inscriptions have been recoverd from different places in Bengal and Bihar speak of the activities of the Buddhists during the twelfth century AD. The text of the Buddhist manuscript[23] named *Pañcarakṣā* was copied in the seventeenth regnal year of Madanapāla.

From these evidences we can conclude that throughout the reign of the Pālas, Buddhism got the royal patronage, though sometimes more and sometimes less, due to certain obvious reasons.

Some other small royal families also contributed a lot to Buddhism by giving patronage to it. A copper-plate inscription of the ninth century AD,[24] revealed the existence of a Buddhist royal family in Harikela. This copper-plate was granted by King Kāntideva of Harikela from the city of Vardhamānapura in Harikela (Sylhet-Comilla-Chittagong region in Bangladesh). Kāntideva is styled *paramasaugata parameśvara* and *mahārājādhirāja*. This record also revealed the names of three successive generations: Bhadradatta, Dhanadatta and Kāntideva. As we have very little information about this dynasty we are not in a position to discuss about the detailed progress, made by Buddhism in this region under this dynasty.

Another dynasty, important from the point of view of Buddhism, was the Candras, who ruled over East Bengal during the period of the Pālas from AD 825 to 1035. The sources of this dynasty include inscriptions belonging to this dynasty, Tibetan chronicles and Tāranātha's accounts. The names of the kings of this dynasty, as revealed from epigraphical records, were : Pūrṇacandra, Suvarṇacandra, Trailokyacandra, Śrīcandra, Kalyāṇacandra, Ladahacandra and Govindacandra.

The Rāmpāl (a place near Dacca) plate of Śrīcandra bearing the *dharmacakra* seal, opens with a verse in honour of Buddha, *Dharma* and *Saṅgha*, says, "Pūrṇacandra's son Suvarṇacandra became a follower of the Buddha".[25] From Suvarṇacandra onwards all the rulers of this dynasty were devout Buddhists, as all the rulers took the title of *paramasaugata* and all the copper-plate grants had on them *dharmacakra* seal.

The patronage of the Pālas no doubt gave an impetus to Buddhism and saved that religion from the fate which overtook in the rest of India. But this did not materially affect the position of the brāhmaṇical religion. This fact is obtained when we notice that the period from eighth to twelfth century AD had more brāhmaṇical images than Buddhist images. Hiuen Tsang mentioned that there were seventy Buddhist *vihāras*, accommodating eight thousand monks and no less than 300 *Deva* temples in Bengal proper. The number of temples and *vihāras* increased many fold during this period. Though the Pāla rulers were Buddhists and their personal inclination was towards Buddhism, they were practical in giving patronage to brāhmaṇical religious faiths along with Buddhism because this was the period of revival of brāhmaṇism. Of the two sects of brāhmaṇism, Vaiṣṇavism seems to have been more popular than Śaivism.

Among the other sects, the *Nirgrantha*s, who later came to be known as Jainas, were very numerous in the days of Hiuen-Tsang. But this sect must have lost its influence to a considerable extent during this period, as we find very few Jaina images and inscriptions to Jaina temples belonging to this period.

But in spite of the existence of different religious sects side by side, there was no sectarian jealousy. This fact of religious toleration of the monarchs of this period is revealed from the various copper-plate inscriptions. Some of the examples of the catholic attitude of the Buddhist kings of the Pāla dynasty and other kings are discussed below.

Nārāyaṇapāla, though a follower of Buddhism, built and endowed a temple of Śiva. He not only attended the sacrificial ceremony of his brāhmaṇa ministers, but also reverently put the sacrificial water on his head.[26] Citramāṭika, the chief queen of Madanapāla regarded it as meritorious to hear the recital of *Mahābhārata*.[27] Similarly Prabhāvatī, queen of Devakhaḍga set up an image of Caṇḍī, a brāhmaṇic diety in her kingdom. On the other hand the Śaiva king Vainyagupta, endowed a Buddhist monastery, while a brāhmaṇa and his wife made pious gifts of land to a Jaina *vihāra*.[28]

This period produced many religious literature belonging to various religions. The literature was both in Sanskrit and Vernacular.

While both Vaiṣṇavism and Śaivism derived their strength and inscription from the magnificent temples, the Buddhists main centres of activity were the numerous *vihāra* or monasteries. We now discuss about some of the Buddhist monasteries and Buddhist centres of activity which prospered in Bengal and Bihar during this period.

Buddhist Centres in Bengal

Tāmralipti

One of the most important centres of Buddhist activities was Tāmralipti, the modern Tāmluk in Midnāpore district of Bengal. This place was (for some time) conquered by the Bhaumakara kings of Orissa, some time in the ninth century AD. But it was recaptured during the Pāla's time and came to be a part of Bengal. Fahien, who resided in this place for a span of two years in the fifth century AD, found Buddhism flourishing with twenty-four monasteries. A terracotta with a relief of Buddha in *bhūmisparśamudrā* and with the Buddhist creed in Gupta characters was found at Panna near Tāmralipti. It was a flourishing Buddhist centre before the Pāla period and contained to be a centre of Buddhist activities during the Pāla's period also.

Bihar-ail

The remains of a brick monastery have been found in the Rājbaḍi mound at Bihar-ail in Rājaśāhī district. It yielded a number of antiquities including a standing image of Buddha of the chunar sand stone, closely similar to the contemporary images of Sārnāth.

Po-shih-po

This monastery, situated three miles west of the capital of Puṇḍra-vardhana, has been found mention in the accounts of Hiuen-Tsang. Near it was an Aśokan tope at the place where Buddha had preached for three months. The establishment was famous for distinguished monks from East India. This place has been identified with the impressive mounds of Bihar and Bhasu-Vihara near Mahāsthāna in the Bogra district of Bangladesh.

Lo-to-Mo-chih

It was stated to have been built by a king in honour of a Buddhist śramaṇa from South India on the victory over a disputant of another system. Hieun-Tsang saw this monastery during his visit to Bengal and mentioned that there were many topes built by Aśoka near this place. *Lo-to-mo-chih* has been translated as *Raktamṛttikā*, the name of which survives in Raṅgamāṭī, a locality near Chiruti in Murśidābād district. The excavation revealed remains of a brick structure which have been supposed to have been a Buddhist establishment of about sixth or seventh century AD. The recent excavations of Rājbaḍiḍongā, one of the mounds of Lo-to-mo-chih yielded a good number of antiquities including bronze images, a seal and sealings with the Buddhist creed, datable to the seventh or eighth centuries AD.

Mi-li-kia-si-kia-po-no or Mṛgasthāpanā in Māldāh

According to I-tsing *mahārājā* Śrī Gupta constructed a temple called 'Temple of China' here for the accommodation of foreign scholars particularly Chinese scholars.

Devaparvata

The Chinese monk Sheng-chi, a contemporary of I-tsing, found four thousand monks and nuns here. The prosperity of this establishment reached its peak under the Buddhist Devas in the eighth-ninth century AD.

Nālandā

This monastic institution, established in the time of Kumāragupta I, became one of the foremost centres of Buddhism during the Pāla period. The excavations revealed a number of monuments including monasteries and *stūpas*. This place was famous not only for providing accommodation to the monks, but also for providing very good education to the Buddhist scholars. The reports of Chinese pilgrims Hiuen-Tsang and I-tsing show the predominance of *Hīnayāna* in the earlier phase but soon *Mahāyāna* and latter *Vajrayāna* occupied predominant place in this institution. Nālandā provided free education in addition to clothes, food, bedding and medicine, to its students. Scholars from different places inside and outside India used to come here to get education. A varieties of subjects including philosophy, law, Sanskrit, Astronomy were studied here. Hiuen-

Tsang reported that about 10,000 students were studying while he visited this place.

Nālandā was damaged by fire during Mahipāla I's reign and was repaired in that year. Like other academic-cum-monastic establishments of the time, Nālandā suffered its end at the hands of Muslim invaders in the beginning of the thirteenth century.

Somapura or Somapuri

This monastery was established during the time of Dharmapāla. It was a residential educational centre where many distinguished scholars from all over the country and outside the country came to study. The ruins of Somapura monastery have been identified with those at Pahārpur in the Rājaśāhī district of Bangladesh. The mound yielded a vast monastic complex consisting of the usual residential cells of monks, places of worship and other structures. This establishement acquired a great sanctity among the Tibetan Buddhists, many of whom undertook pilgrimage to this place. The great Buddhist scholar Atiśa-Dipaṅkara resided here when he translated into Tibetan, in collaboration with others, the *Mādhyamakaratnapradīpa* of Bhāvaviveka.[29] About the middle of the eleventh century this *vihāra* was set on fire by the armies of south east Bengal. Though it was renovated by a monk Vipulasmṛtimitra, it could not be restored to its former glory. The actual reason for the downfall of this great monastic institution is not known. The remnants of Somapura Mahāvihāra do not bear any large scale vandalism. It is in all probability that the Buddhist monks abandoned this place at the time of Muslim invasion and took shelter in Nepal and Tibet.

Vikramaśilā

Another monastic-cum-academic establishment, built during the reign of Dharmapāla, was Vikramaśilā *mahāvihāra*. The location of the site has been a subject of controversy among scholars. According to Sumpa[30] this *vihāra* was situated to the east of Magadha. Tāranātha[31] locates it on the precipitious hill in Magadha on the right bank of the Ganges. But the most recent view is that the place Antichak, in the district of Bhāgalpur in

Bihar is the most probable site of this *mahāvihāra*.

The University Campus comprised of six Colleges with 108 *puṇḍits*. One of the most distinguished scholars of this monastery was Dipaṅkara Srijñāna. The popularity of painting in this *vihāra* has been indicated by a twelfth-century inscription[32] recently discovered which gives hints of construction of two *caityas* here.

The subjects like logic, grammer, metaphysics, ritualistic practices etc. were taught here. There was provision for the award of diploma to the monk students who showed proficiency. Students not only from India but also from Tibet and Nepal came to study here. Many Sanskrit texts were translated into Tibetan in this centre.

Like other institutions of this time, this monastery was also destroyed by Muslim Vandals.

Odantapura or Odantapuri

We know very little about this monastery as the site has not been unearthed yet. It is believed that the site was in the vicinity of Bihar-shariff. The Tibetan sources say that Gopāla, established this monastery in the vicinity of Nālandā[33] and this monastery contained 12,000 inmates which is a indication of its prosperity under the Pālas.[34] On the model of Odantapura *mahāvihāra*, the first Tibetan Buddhist monastery Sam-ye was built in AD 749.

Nag-tsho, a Tibetan monk who visited India towards the end of the eleventh century mentioned that there were only fiftythree monks in Odantapura monastery which is a clear indication of its decline by that time.[35]

Jagaddala

The magnificent *vihāra* of Jagaddala, a creation of Rāmapāla was the last glory of Buddhism in ancient Bengal. Sandhyākara Nandi mentions in his book *Rāmacarita* that this *mahavihāra* was located at Rāmāvati in Varendri in north Bengal.[36] But the exact location of this monastery has been a problem to scholars. It may be located in the village named

Jagadala, four miles south-east of Bamangaon in the Māldāh district of West-Bengal.[37] Indo-Tibetan cultural intercourse reached its high stage during this period as a large number of original and Tibetan translation of the Sanskrit works were done here. This fact has been provided by Tibetan scholars Bstan-hgyur and Bkagyur.

The monastery lost its glory due to the Muslim invasion as many inmates of this monastery fled to Nepal, Arakan and other places for safety.

Maināmati (Paṭṭikera)

One of the largest centres of Buddhism in Bengal came to light just by an accident. It was discovered on a slope of a mound known as Sālbanpur mound, in the Maināmati Lalmai region, five miles west of Comilla in Bangladesh. The excavations have revealed the remains of a 550 ft square Buddhist monastery at a place called Sālban *vihāra*. Three distinctive levels of construction, now exposed to view, reveal that the *vihāra* belonging to different periods, and it enjoyed the patronage of different dynasties. A terracotta sealing with the legend *śrī-bhāvadeva mahāvihāra-ārya-bhikṣu-saṅghasya* found in the ruins of the first period indicates that Śrī Bhābhadeva, the founder ruler of the Deva dynasty, who resigned in the eighth century AD, was the founder of this monastery.

The treasures of Sālban *vihāra* unearthed by archaeologists include *inter alia*, copper-plates, silver coins, terracotta plaques, seals and sealings, gold ornaments, silver ingots and images of Buddha and Buddhist deities like Tārā and Bodhisattvas Padmapāṇi.

Paṭṭikera, by the side of the Maināmati hill, was once a great centre of Buddhist learning before the eleventh century, is attested by the painting of a sixteen-armed Cuṇḍā with the legend *paṭṭikera cuṇḍāvara-bhavane cuṇḍa* on a manuscript of the *Aṣṭasāhasrika Prajñāpāramitā*, copied in the year AD 1015.[38] The donor is described as proficient in the rites of the *Sahaja* cult (a late Tāntric Buddhist sect).

Besides these important Buddhist monasteries, there were many minor monasteries which came into prominence due to the patronage of the Pāla rulers. Some of these monasteries are mentioned in the following lines.

Devīkoṭa or Devakoṭa

It was located in ancient Puṇḍravardhanabhukti. The ruins of a medieval city called Diw-koṭ identical with Devīkoṭa, found about eighteen miles south of the Dinājpur town in the village of Bangarh, supposedly include the site of this monastery.[39]

Paṇḍita

It was located in Chittagong of Bangladesh. It was a notable centre of Tāntric Buddhism which had a magnificent temple within its enclosure.[40]

Sannagar

It was reportedly located in East Bengal, but its exact location has not yet been ascertained. It was a very important seat of Buddhists during the Pāla period.

Vikramapura or Vikramapuri

It was situated in Bengal towards the east of Magadha and its Origin has been connected with Dharmapāla.[41]

Bharatour

This place is found mention in the accounts of the Chinese pilgrims and indigenous writings. It was located near the Panagarh Railway station in the Burdwan district of West Bengal from where a monastery complex with brick built *stūpa* and a number of beautiful figures of Buddha in *bhumisparśamudrā* were found.

Traikūṭaka

It is located in Rāḍhā in Bengal where Haribhadra is said to have written his famous commentary on the *Abhisamayālaṅkārikā* under the patronage of Dharmapāla.[42]

Besides these *vihāras*, there were many more *vihāras* or Buddhist centres in Bengal and Bihar about which our knowledge is not sufficient due to lack of proper materials.

Now we will discuss in brief about the great patrons of Buddhism in the Pāla dynasty of Bengal.

Patrons

Gopāla I

Nothing is definitely known about the history of Bengal in the period between the death of Harṣavardhan and the rise of the Pālas. This was a period of anarchy, foreign invasion and misrule ending the rule of the old royal dynasty. It was a glorious moment in history when the chiefs, unable to deal with the existing chaotic political situation agreed to elect Gopāla, the son of a successful soldier Vapyaṭa, as the ruler of the whole of Bengal and Bihar. In the Khālimpur grant of Dharmapāla, it is said[43] that the people made Gopāla take the hand of fortune. Unfortunately nothing more is known about this great incident of history.

Gopāla I probably ascended the throne in about AD 750. But scholars differ about the exact date of his accession. Most probably Gopāla I was an elderly man when he was called to the throne. Nothing is definitely known about the events of his reign. According to Lāmā Tāranātha, Gopāla built the celebrated monastery at Odantapura in Bihar[44] and he was a pious Buddhist. It is said that Gopāla was a devotee and bane factor of Buddhism.[45] He revived the Nālandā monastery, erected several new monasteries in his dominion and offered lavish gifts to the Buddhsit clergy.[46]

Dharmapāla

Dharmapāladeva, the son and successor of Gopāla I was the real founder of the Pāla dynasty as he consolidated the empire with a great skill. Like his father he was a great Buddhist. He is credited with the foundation of the celebrated Vikramaśilā monastery in the Bhāgalpur district of Bihar. This monastery had 107 temples and six colleges. Dharmapāla made

Haribhadra, a great commentator of the *Prajñāpāramitā-sūtra*, his spiritual preceptor. Tāranātha is of the opinion that the teachings of the *Prajñāpāramitā* spread widely under the auspices of this king.[47]

Devapāla

Dharmapāla was succeeded by his able son Devapāla, who further pushed his kingdom as far as the Himālayas in the North and the Vindhya Hills in the south. This fact is corroborated by the Bādāl Pillar Inscription.[48] From the copper-plate discoverd at Nālandā,[49] it appears that Devapāla granted five villages for various comforts of the Vikshus as well as for writing the *Dharmaratnas* and for the upkeep of the Buddhist monastery, built there by Bālaputradeva, the king of Suvarṇadvīpa and Yava Bhumi (Jāvā-Sumātrā). Devapāla constructed many Buddhist temples and monasteries in Magadha. Thus Buddhist art and architecture got a fresh impetus during the reign of Devapāla.

After the death of Devapāla there was political instability in Bengal for some time and some weak rulers succeeded the throne one after another. Though these kings were devout Buddhists, they could hardly get time to propagate this faith, as they were busy in maintaining political stability.

Nārāyaṇapāla

The most notable king after the death of Devapāla was Nārāyāṇapāla. In the Bhāgalpur copper-plate of the reign of Nārāyaṇapāla, the king is mentioned as a devotee to *sugata*.[50] A small inscription of Nārāyaṇapāla was found by Pandit V.V. Vidya Vinoda in the Inscriptions Gallery of Indian Museum, Calcutta, which was published in the *Journal of the Vangiya-Sāhitya Pariṣad* (*JVSP*).[51] It records the erection of an image of Buddha in the ninth regnal year of the king Nārāyaṇapāla, by a Buddhist Elder Dharmamitra, an inhabitant of Andhra country in the month of *Baiśākha*.

Gopāla II

Another notable King of the Pāla dynasty was Gopāla II. The British

Museum possesses a manuscript of the *Aṣṭasāhasrikā Prajñāpāramitā* written in the fifteenth regnal year of Gopāla II at the Vikramaśilā Monastery.

Mahipāla I

From the Buddhism point of view the reign of Mahipāla I, another ruler of the Pāla dynasty, was an important one. In the seventeenth year of his reign, an image of Buddha was dedicated in or near the temple of the Mahābodhi at Bodh Gayā and in the same year the temple at Nālandā was restored, as it was burnt down in a fire.[52] Under the orders of the king the wheels of Law at Banāras was being repaired and a new temple (*Gandhakuṭi*) built by the brothers Sthirapāla and Vasantapāla.[53] According to Tāranatha, Mahipāla reigned for fiftytwo years, which is most probably correct as the Imadpur images were dedicated in the 48th year of the king. The long reign of Mahipāla I is important from the point of issuing a large number of inscriptions and manuscript records. The manuscript of *Aṣṭasāhasrikā Prajñāpāramitā*, now in the University Library at Cambridge is the work of Mahipāla's time.

Rāmapāla

The reign of Rāmapāla, a Pāla ruler, was important from the point of Buddhism. He founded a new city named Rāmāvatī which had a Buddhist *vihāra* named Jagaddala *mahāvihāra*. One of the Rāmapāla's records named Tetrāwān Image Inscription, recorded the erection of an image of Tārā by a certain Bhaṭṭa Icchāra in the second year of the king's reign.[54]

Govindapāla

The last important Pāla King, who was recognised by the Buddhists as a great patron of Buddhism was Govindapāladeva. He took the title *paramasaugata* which clearly gives impression of his faith in Buddhism. His end in AD 1199 was practically the end of Buddhism in Bengal, though the faith continued as a lesser spiritual force till the invasion of the Muslims.

It is significant to note that though most of the kings of the Pāla dynasty were followers of Buddhism, they were never orthodox or sectarian. Their religious belief did not influence the policy of the state, which was based on long running traditions. This fact is corroborated from the long list of brāhmaṇa Prime Ministers under the Buddhist Pāla Kings. All the epigraphic records now show that the rulers of this dynasty endowed both the Buddhist and brāhmaṇical temples and establishments. This fact prove beyond doubt about the catholic nature of the Pāla rulers.

BHAUMAKARA AGE

In the history of Buddhism, particularly of *Mahāyāna* and *Vajrayāna* Buddhism in Orissa, the rise of the Bhaumakaras in the first half of the eighth century AD was most significant. The Bhaumakara rulers extended whole-hearted royal patronage to this religion and saved it from its total extinction. The legends, traditions, monuments several copper-plate inscriptions attest to the flourishing condition of Buddhism during the rule of the Bhaumakaras.

Due to the efforts of the Bhauma Kings, Buddhism reached the pinnacle of its glory in Orissa. This was a period when Buddhism transformed itself from Mahāyānism to Vajrayānism in Orissa. There was a phenomenal growth of Vajrayānism in this period. Although the records of the Bhauma monarchs leave no room for doubt about their adherence to Buddhism, but they do not reveal much about their activities in furtherance of their faith.

The Neulpur charter[55] says that the first three kings of the Bhaumakara dynasty Kṣemaṅkara, Śivakara I, and Śubhakara I were staunch supporters of Buddhism as they bore Buddhist epithets before their names. The Dhenkanāl plate of Tribhuvana Mahādevī says that Tribhuvana Mahādevī's predecssors were Buddhists and they exhausted the vast treasure of the kingdom for the cause of Buddhism.[56] The inscription of Bhimata[57] from Gaṇeśa Gumphā of Udayagiri which records that all the caves of the Kumārī hill in Udayagiri had been occupied by the Buddhist monks by the end of the eighth century AD.

While editing the Khadipaḍā image inscription, A. Ghose has suggested that there was a state pontiff of Buddhism under the Bhaumakaras, as in the above-mentioned inscription there is the mention of a *mahāmaṇḍalācārya* and *paramaguru*, that is teacher of the great division and supreme preceptor respectively.[58] It is not yet clear whether the Bhauma rulers, who were great advocates of religious toleration, ever used their bureaucratic machinery for religious propagation. But it is very clear that Buddhism flourished in a great extent in Orissa, only due to the religious zeal of the Bhauma monarchs.

The whole kingdom of the Bhaumas was adorned with a large number of monastic institutions. These monasteries were academic-cum-religious institutions. They were adorned with superb images of Buddha, and different icons of the Mahāyānic and Vajrayānic pantheons. These monasteries were seats of culture and education which taught both religious as well as secular education. The teachers were greatly loved and respected by all the people because of their deep knowledge on the subjects, they taught. In course of time some of the monasteries grew up into famous universities and as torch bearers of the Buddhist culture they attracted pupils and scholars not only from India but also from many foreign countries.

Buddhist Centres

Here we now discuss briefly about some of the Buddhist centres in Orissa which flourished during the time of the Bhaumakara rule.

Ratnagiri

The famous Buddhist centre is situated on an insolated hill of the Āsiā Range in Jājpur sub-division in the district of Cuttack in Orissa. It is remarkable by its rich antiquities consisting of the colossal statues of Buddha, Bodhisattvas, Tārās and various Tāntric deities executed in graceful style, which may well be classified among the finest creation of Indian art.[59] Ratnagiri was a famous centre of learning. Both secular and Buddhist teachings were given to the students of this centre. By eighth century AD, it was developed to its fullness, though it was started some time before this period.

Tāranātha tells us that towards the end of the reign of a king named Buddhapākṣa, a monastery called Ratnagiri was built in Orissa in the cleft of a mountain near the sea.[60] The Tibetan historian further informs us that in that *vihāra* were kept three copies of each of the *Hīnayāna* and *Mahāyāna* texts as well as *Śāstras*. He again informs that the king established eight great centres for Buddhist doctrines and there were five hundred Buddhist monks there. The King Buddha Pākṣa of Tāranātha, has been identified with Gupta emperor Narasiṁha Bālāditya. Thus it seems that during the Gupta rule of Orissa, this famous monastery was built. The existing *stūpa* of Ratnagiri appears to have been built over an earlier edifice belonging to the Gupta period, because on the midst of the debris has been discovered a stone slab inscribed with the *Pratīyasamutpāda sūtra*, in the characters of the Gupta period. Thus it appears certain that Ratnagiri monastery was built first during the reign of Narasiṁhagupta Bālāditya, some time between the fifth century AD and early sixth century AD.

In the Nāgārjunakoṇḍa inscription, as well as in the accounts of Hiuen-Tsang, we get the reference to a monastery called Puṣpagiri *vihāra*. The Nāgārjunakoṇḍa inscription states that *upāsikā* Bodhi-Śrī constructed a Sailamaṇḍapa at Puṣpagiri.[61] The accounts of Hiuen-Tsang says, "In the south-west of the country was the *Pu-si-po-ki-li* monastery in a mountain, the stone tope of this monastery exhibited supernatural lights and other miracles.[62] Julien has restored 'Pu-si-po-ki-li' as Puṣpagiri.[63] Unfortunately the location of this site has not been settled unanimously as scholars vary in their identification. R.L. Mitra[64] identifies Puṣpagiri with Dhaulī, whereas N.K. Sahu[65] locates it in the Phūlbani district of Ghumsur region of Orissa. Another two famous historians R.P. Chanda[66] and R.D. Banerji[67] identify Puṣpagiri with Ratnagiri, which is situated to the south-west of Jājpur. This identification seems to be acceptable to many, because of the extensiveness of the remains of the area of Ratnagiri.

From the Tibetan records we come to know that Ratnagiri was a famous centre for *Yoga* during our period of study. The Tibetan records[68] say that two famous Buddhist scholars Bodhi-Śrī and Naropa practised *Yoga* at Ratnagiri in Orissa. They further inform that great teachers and *ācāryas* resided here to teach *Yoga* and philosophy to scholars, coming from the different parts of the country. Lāmā Tāranātha[69] informs that Ācārya Pito, who had acquired the *siddhi* of invisibility, was a renowned teacher of *Yoga* at Ratnagiri. Probably in this monastery the famous *Mahāyāna* Buddhist scholar Prajñā had studied *Yoga*.[70] According to Tibetan sources Ratnagiri was noted for pursuit of *Kālacakra-tantra* in the later part of the tenth century AD.

The excavations at Ratnagiri laid bare the remains of two imposing quadrangular monasteries, an imposing *stūpa*, a single-winged monastery, eight temples, a large number of small votive *stūpas* and a large number of Buddhist sculptures and objects of daily use. From the epigraphical point of view we can assign this establishment to the Bhaumakara period.[71]

A large head of Buddha, found on the slope of the hill and another on the tope of the hill indicate the colossal nature of their original images. The Tārā images of Ratnagiri in *tribhaṅga* poses, are exquisitely charming. Many Bodhisattva images, were found from this sight. Many of the sculptures also bear the reliefs of divinities of the *Vajrayāna* pantheon.

The remnants of Ratnagiri is an adequate index of the profound popularity and the sanctity of the centre in the Buddhist world during the Bhaumakara period.

Lalitagiri or Nalatigiri

Lalitagiri, a part of Āsiā Range Hill, in the Birupā-Chitratpalā Valley, near to Ratnagiri, is one of the major centres of Buddhism in Orissa. Several Buddhist images, assigned to eighth to tenth centuries AD have been discovered from this site. The Buddhist images include statues of Buddha, Bodhisattvas, Tārās, and *Vajrayāna* images. The images of Avalokiteśvara, Mañjuśrī, Maitreya, Tārā, Prajñā and above all Buddha in different *mudrās* particularly one in *bhūmisparśamudrā* are carved out in beautiful style.

The excavations at Lalitagiri conducted by ASI under Prof. K.S. Behera, an eminent historian and others reveal the remains of a massive *stūpa* with Buddhist relics found in three caskets. The caskets are made up of gold, silver and stealite, put into each other respectively. In the innermost casket, i.e., in the gold casket, a tooth relic has been found.

Though there is no direct evidence as to who the founders of this establishment were, it is in all probability that the Bhauma kings are involved with the construction of the *stūpa*.

The existence of atleast one imposing monastery can be surmised from the sculptured door jams found in the Lalitagiri, resembling that of Ratnagiri. Various *Māhāyāna* and *Vajrayāna* images, found from this site, are made of local sandstones. Excavations still are going on under the guidance of ASI, which in future, may make our knowledge about this Buddhist site more concrete.

Udayagiri

It forms the easternmost peak of the Āsiā Range, on the side of the Birupā river, about seven miles from Lalitagiri. The site exposes many beautifully carved images of Buddha, Bodhisattvas, Tārās and some *Vajrayāna* deities.

The most remarkable figure found here is the image of four-armed Avalokiteśvara of the Jaṭāmukuṭa type. It was from this site that the beautiful door-frame was removed by John Beams to Patna Museum along with a few large sized Buddhist images.

The existence of a *stūpa* can be traced from the ruins in the form of brick mounds on the western side of the Udayagiri hill. The most interesting images of this site were seated Dhyāni Buddha Amitāva, twelve-armed Prajñāpāramitā, and Jaṭāmukuṭa Lokeśvara.

From the discovery of a large number of sculptures from this site, it becomes clear that it remained an important Buddhist centre during the rule of the Bhaumakaras.

Jājpur

Jājpur, popularly known as the Virajākṣetra, on the Vaitaraṇī river, is about 80 kms from Cuttack, in the south-eastern direction. It is the place from where the Bhaumakaras and some other ruling families ruled Orissa.

The most noteworthy discovery of this place is the four images of the Bodhisattvas, which are now found within the compound of the S.D.O office Jājpur. These excellent images were carved very beautifully.

Many other Buddhist centres had developed near Jājpur during the Bhaumakara period. Prominent among them are Dharmaśālā, Kendrāparā, Bānesvaranāsi, Chauduār, Kuṇḍeśvara, Prāchi Valley, all in the district of Cuttack, Ayodhyā, Khaḍipaḍā, Kupari in the Bālāsore district and Tālcher in the Dhenkanāl district. Many *Mahāyāna* and *Vajrayāna* images of exquisite quality have come to light from these sites.

Dhaulī or Tosāli

Tosāli or Dhaulī assumed importance and celebrity in the Buddhist world, since the time of Aśoka and continued to be a famous centre of Buddhism for several centuries thereafter. The Dhaulī cave inscription of the time of Śāntikara I reveals that a monastery named Arghyakava-ratika was constructed in AD 829 by Bhimata and Bhatta Lo Yamaka.[72] The Nāgārjunakoṇḍa inscription refers to the *Thera* School of Tosāli, whereas *Gaṇḍavyūha* reflects the Mahāyānic importance of the place. From these evidences we can assume that both the Hīnayānism and Mahāyānism prevailed in Dhaulī.

The Udayagiri cave inscription of the time of Śāntikara I, incised by Bhimata[73] led us to believe that all the caves of the Udayagiri hill were occupied by the Buddhist monks in the Bhaumakara period. This fact proved beyond doubt that both the hills of Dhaulī and Udayagiri were strong holds of Buddhism in this period.

Cheli-ta-lo

This was a famous port on the Orissa coast, flourishing at the time of Yuan Chwang's visit. According to Yuan Chwang the city was situated to the south-east of Wu-tu country and was a remarkable seat of *Mahāyāna* Buddhism.[74] The pilgrim found the city sorrounded by strong and lofty walls outside which there were five great convents with many storeyed towers. All these five convents were full of life and each of them was adorned with artistic carvings of Buddha and Bodhisattva images.[75] The pilgrime floated his thought that standing on the shore, in a clear star-lit night, beyond the sea he could perceive at a great distance the glittering rays of the precious gem placed on the top of the *stūpa* of the tooth of Buddha.[76]

Unfortunately the identification of this place is yet a disputed question. The great archaeologist Cunningham[77] restores the word *Che-li-ta-lo* into Charitrapur and identified it with the present town of Purī, whereas De Weddel[78] suggests the place to be near Chitrotpāla river.

Jayasrama Monastery

It was situated to the north of Tosāli and was in a flourishing condition during the reign of the Bhaumakaras. The Bhauma king Śivakaradeva III, at the request of Ranaka Vinitatunga, executed a copper-plate grant in AD 885, allotting the revenue of the village Kallani for the god Buddha Bhaṭṭāraka, whose sanctuary lay with this monastery.[79]

Kurumā

Kurumā, about five miles from Koṇārka in the district of Purī, was an important Buddhist centre during the time of Bhaumakaras of Orissa. The excavation at Kurumā revealed a Buddhist complex with a *stūpa* and several Buddhist images datable to the tenth century AD. From the excavated area have been found red ware pottery of the tenth century character and a circular terracotta tablet upon which is engraved a Buddhist *Dhāraṇī* datable to the tenth century AD.[80]

Achutarājpur (Bāṇapur)

Achutarājpur, in Bāṇapur, in the district of Purī deserves special mention, as this site has yielded the richest hoard of bronze images in Orissa. This hoard, found in three earthen pots contained several figures, seventeen *stūpas*, a bell, a spouted pot, all made up of bronze. The total number of bronze figures is ninetyfive from which seventyfive are Buddhist images. Besides the figure of Buddha, there were more than a dozen Buddhist deities like Avalokiteśvara, Vajrasattva, Heruka and other *Mahāyāna* and *Vajrayāna* images.

These bronze images are very interesting not only for their artistic qualities, but also from iconographical point of view. It seems that this place was initially a Mahāyānic centre but in course of time became a strong centre of *Vajrayāna*.[81]

A Tārā image of this site contains the inscription *Gauriputta Saṅgha* which makes us believe that probably a Buddhist *saṅgha* existed here in the time of Bhauma ruler Gaurī Mahadevī.[82]

The Bāṇapur site came to the notice of the public when the work for a college building had begun in 1963. The site has been practically levelled down for the purpose of the college building, thus destroying a great Buddhist establishment. The clearance of 1963 yielded a lifesize head of Buddha, a large stone pedestal, a relief of a *stūpa* and a large number of fragmented sculptures.

According to N.K. Sahu,[83] the image, worshipped at present as Tārini in Bāṇapur, is that of goddess Tārā, as after the decline of Buddhism most of the Buddhist images were converted into non-Buddhist gods and goddess.

Baud

It is a great centre of *Mahāyāna* and Tāntric Buddhism during the Bhaumakara period. Situated in the district of Phūlbani, this place has a temple called Rāmeśvara temple. The compound of the temple is sorrounded by a large number of Buddhist figures both *Mahāyāna* and Tāntric. Many of the figures are either broken or covered with thick layers or vermilion making it very difficult to recognise. Prof. R.D. Banerji[84] is of the opinion that Buddhism lingered longer in Baud than in other parts of Orissa.

Khiching

Khiching, the ancient Khijiṅgakoṭṭa (the capital of the Bhañjas) in the district of Mayūrbhanj, was once a great centre of Buddhism. A haphazard digging in the mound Varatgarh in this place, has exposed the remnants of a brick quadrangular structure which looks like a Buddhist monastery. This idea of a monastery has been strengthened by the discovery of six terracotta plaques, from this site now placed in the Khiching and Bāripada museum, each with the relief of a *stūpa*.[85]

The noted discoveries of this place include Buddha in Bhūmisparśamudrā, Mañjuśrī, Mārici, Vasudhara, Jambhala, Tārā, Vajrasattva and Lokeśvara. These images were found from the Sankhurajagarh, Kukuḍāgarh and Varatgarh mounds of Khiching.

All these images show beyond doubt the importance of Khiching in the Buddhist world particularly from the point of view of Vajrayānism.

Besides the above-mentioned Buddhist sites, there existed many other Buddhist centres in Orissa, about which we have very little knowledge due to non-availability of materials.

We are now going to discuss in brief about some of the important rulers of the Bhaumakara dynasty in Orissa, who gave patronage to Buddhism.

Patrons

The most glorious period in the history of Buddhism in Orissa was the period of the Bhaumakaras. The contribution of the Bhaumakara dynasty to the propagation and spread of Buddhism is uncomparable. No other dynasty in Orissa has done so much for the Buddhist faith, as compared to the Bhaumakaras.

The first group the Bhuma kings were devout Buddhists and tried their best to make this religion a great force.

Kṣemaṅkaradeva

The first king of the Bhaumakara dynasty Kṣemaṅkaradeva ruled from AD 736 to 756, Neulpur plate[86] of Śubhakaradeva I, the grandson of Kṣemaṅkaradeva, represents Kṣemaṅkara as *paramopāsakānugata*, i.e., the follower of the great worshipper of Lord Buddha. According to the Tibetan tradition he was converted to Buddhism by Tibetan monk Luipa.[87] Though Kṣemaṅkara was a staunch follower of Buddhism he established four orders (caste) in their proper place.[88] Buddhism which was against caste system could not prevail upon him regarding this matter. Here we find an interesting example of a Buddhist ruler propagating the caste system, disregarding the Buddhist teachings.

Śivakaradeva I (*alias* Unmatta Siṁha)

Śivakara I, the son and successor of Kṣemaṅkara ruled from AD 756 to 790. The Neulpur plate of his son Śubhakaradeva I mentions Śivakara I as a *parama tathāgata*, i.e., the devout worshipper of the *tathāgata* or Buddha.[89] It was a period when Buddhist Tāntric sect was beginning to dominate Orissa. Śivakara I sent in AD 795 to Te-tsang, the emperor of China, as present, the autographed manuscript of the *Gaṇḍavyūha*, the last section of the *Boddhā vā-taṁsa*, dealing with the practice and vow of Bodhisattva Sāmantabhadra.[90] He also instructed Prajñā, a scholar on *Mahāyāna* to supply the translation of the *Mahāyāna* text to Te-tsang. In this period the great monastery of Ratnagiri had become a centre of Buddhist religion and learning. *Tantras* and *Yoga* were the principal subjects of this centre.

Śivakara I's period was very important as in this period the cultural contact with China became possible through the gift of a Buddhist text.

Śubhakaradeva I

The third king of this dynasty Śubhakaradeva I bears the title *paramasaugata*, i.e., a devout Buddhist.[91] Śubhakaradeva I was a great patron of Buddhism. The Baud plate of Pṛthvīmahādevī[92] credits him with the erection of a number of Buddhist *vihāras*. According to the Khadipada image Inscription, Śubhakara I installed an Avalokiteśvara image.[93] Though a Buddhist, Śubhakara I allowed his queen Mādhavīdevī to be a worshipper of Lord Śiva, which shows his catholicity towards other religions.

Śivakara II

From the Terundia plate of his son Śubhakara II, it is known that Śivakara II was a *saugatāsrava* or one who seeks refuge in the *saugata*

(Buddha).[94] This fact shows his devotion to Buddhism. Till the end of his rule, i.e., AD 829, he tried his best for the furtherance of Buddhist religion.

Śāntikaradeva I

Śāntikaradeva I succeeded his elder brother Śivakara II in AD 829 and ruled till AD 836. The Gaṇesa Guṁphā inscription[95] of Śāntikaradeva I, in the hills of Udayagiri, incised by Bhimata, make us believe that many Buddhist monks were staying in the caves of this hill during this period. This example proves beyond doubt about the flourishing condition of Buddhism during the period of Śāntikaradeva I.

Śubhakaradeva II

Like his father, Śubhakaradeva II also took the title of *paramasaugata* or devout worshipper of Buddha.[96] The Tirunḍia grant informs us that Śubhakaradeva II established, like his great grandfather Kṣemaṅkara, the order of the *varṇāśrama* or caste system.[97] But his devotion to Buddhism was unquestionable as we find a lot of Buddhist monuments, belonging to his period.

After the death of Śubhakaradeva II in AD 839 we see a series of rulers belonging to the Bhauma dynasty ruling over Orissa. They were Śubhakaradeva III, Tribhuvana Mahādevī I, Śāntikaradeva II, Śubhakara deva IV, Sivakaradeva III, Pṛthvī Mahādevī *alias* Tribuvana Mahādevī II, Śāntikaradeva III, Śubhakaradeva V, Gaurī Mahādevī, Daṇḍī Mahādevī, Vakula Mahādevī and Dharma Mahādevī. These rulers were able to rule till the end of the first half of tenth century AD. Though these rulers did not attach the Buddhist titles to their names, as done by their forefathers, they did not do anything against the Buddhist religion. Rather the support to the monasteries and to the Buddhists continued unhampered during the rule of the later Bhauma rulers.

The Bhauma monarchs, particularly the first group of rulers, were keen followers of Buddhism and they erected a number of Buddhist structures on their kingdom, the remnants of which are still lying in most parts of Orissa.

Although most of the Bhaumakara rulers were devout Buddhists, they were never sectarian or orthodox. Because of this unorthodox nature of the ruling family, diverse sects existed in Orissa simultaneously. Wide and sympathetic toleration was the general characteristic of our period. It seems that there was no cultural difference between different religious sects and that is why the rulers found it possible to support all sects.

Though Buddhism was the most dominant religion of this period in Orissa, the presence of Jainism, Śaivism and Vaiṣṇavism etc. were also felt to some extent.

We see that Jainism existed in Orissa with very low popular support during this period. We also have evidence to prove that after the decline of the Bhaumakara dynasty in the tenth century AD, Buddhism suffered a great set back. Śaivism and Vaiṣṇavism became popular due to the patronage of the Somavaṁśīs and Gaṅga rulers just after the rule of the Bhaumakaras. Even during the rule of the Bhaumakaras, Śaivism was very much present in Orissa. Mādhavīdevī, wife of Śubhakara I of the Bhauma dynasty constructed a Śaiva temple and enshrined Mādhaveśvara in it after her name. This fact has been corroborated from the Haṁśesvara temple inscription.[98] We find the figures of the couchant bull, the symbol of the Śaivites on the seals attached to most of the Bhaumakara copper-plates. This fact makes us more certain that the Bhauma rulers held Śaivism in high esteem. P. Mukherji[99] is of the opinion that the later Bhauma rulers might have been influenced by the visit of Śaṅkarācārya, one of the greatest propagator of Hinduism (Śaiva sect), to Purī in the ninth century AD. From the Hindol plate of Śubhakaradeva III,[100] a ruler of the Bhauma dynasty we come to know that a village was gifted for the worship of Lord Śiva.

Vaiṣṇavism, which had its glorious days prior to the Bhaumakara, suffered a set back in the seventh century AD, due to the popularity of Buddhism but again became a force during the later Bhaumakara period. The Dhenkanāl plate[101] of a ruler of the Bhaumakara dynasty Tribhuvana Mahādevī I describes her as *Parama Vaiṣṇavī*. The Baud plate of Pṛthvī Mahādevī,[102] another Bhauma ruler speaks of the donor as *Parama Vaiṣṇavī*.

Among the feudatories of the Bhaumas, the Bhañjas seemed to profess devotion to Vaiṣṇavism, as their grants have been recorded on the occasion of *Visuvasaṅkrānti*, *Devotsānadvādasī*, and other Vaiṣṇavite days.

The cult of Śakti was engulfing the whole of India at that time and Orissa could not isolate herself from this. Tribhuvana Mahādevī I, in her Dheṅkanāl character,[103] compares hereself with Kātyāyani, which is identified with goddess Virajā, a symbol of *śakti* (strength). Virajākṣetra (i.e., Jājpur) became a centre of Śakti cult during the later half of the Bhauma rule, as a number of Mātrika images like Cāmuṇḍā belonging to the later Bhauma period have been discovered at Jājpur and its sorrounding areas. Another important centre of the Śakti cult during this period was Bhubaneśvar. According to K.C. Panigrahi[104] a great historian, the Śākta temple of Vaitāla in Bhubaneśvar, which has Cāmuṇḍā as the presiding deity, was constructed during the Bhaumakara period. Many other Śākta temples are found even now in Bhubaneśvar, from which some were constructed during the Bhaumakara period.

The period from eighth to twelfth century AD in Orissa is unique in the sense that all the major religious beliefs like Buddhism, Śaivism, Vaiṣṇavism and Śāktism seem to have synthesised into a cosmopolitan form, losing their separate entities. This period also saw a great transformation in Buddhism. Vajrayānism made a great headway during this period, eclipsing Mahāyānism.

EVOLUTION OF BUDDHISM

The outlook and character of Buddhism have changed radically during the period of our study. This was the period when Tāntrism developed. Buddhism has passed through conceptual, ritualistic and organisational change. The simplicity of the religion has been replaced by a complex character. This period was a landmark so far as the evolution of Buddhism is concerned.

After the demise of Buddha, Buddhism was divided into two distinct sects one *Hīnayāna* or *Theravāda* Buddhists and the second *Mahāsāṅghikas*, who later got the name *Mahāyāna*. Again *Mahāyāna* philosophy has two schools known as *Mādhyamika* and *Yogācāra*. In the seventh and eighth centuries both *Mādhyamika* and *Yogācāra* lost their original vigour and an attempt was made to synthesise the two by Śāntarakṣita, Kamalaśīla and Haribhadra. About the same time a new form of Buddhism was developed under the name *Tantrayāna* or Mystic

Buddhism. It is believed that the Buddhist *Mahāyāna* based on *tantras* originated in Andhra in the sixth century AD. It was expressed in three forms of mystic practices, i.e., *Vajrayāna*, *Kālacakrayāna* and *Sahajayāna*. The teachers of *tāntrika* school are called *siddhas* or *siddhācāryas* and thier number is eightyfour according to the Indian and Tibetan sources. These *siddhas* mostly hailed from Magadha and Bengal. Most of their works are preserved in Tibetan translations. Among important books may be maintained the names of *Guhyasamāja-tantra*, *Kālacakra- tantra* and *Saṁvara-tantra*.[105] Several Sanskrit tāntric texts in Oriya script namely *Kaulacūḍāmaṇi* and the *Vārāhi Tantra* can be ascribed to the ninth-tenth century AD.

Tantrayāna Buddhism is fundamentally affiliated to Hindu Tantrism as it aims at reaching the state of non-duality by destroying all forms of dualism. Two aspects viz. the negative and the positive, the static and the dynamic are essential features of Tantrism. The *tāntrika* Buddhists conceive the negative and the static as the female *prajñā* and the positive and the dynamic as the male *upāya*, while the Hindu *tāntrikas* designate them respectively as Śakti and Śiva, but differ from their Buddhist counterpart in regarding the female as the positive and the dynamic and the male as the negative and static. The *tāntrika* Buddhists believe that the union of *prajñā* and *upāya*, leads to the annihilation of all principles of dualism and the final stage of non-duality, the Absolute Being, the state of *Yuganaddha*, comparable to that of *advaya*, *maithuna*, *samarasa* of other esoteric systems. One who reaches the stage of *Yuganaddha* gets supreme bliss (*mahāsukha*), perfect enlightenment and eternal tranquillity and has crossed the sea of birth and death and it is in this manner countless Buddhas have attained perfection. According to the Tāntric Buddhists Gautama was the incarnation of *upāya* and his wife Gopā that of *prajñā* and due to the union of these two Gautama got *mahāsukha* of the nature of *Nirvāṇa*. The union of *prajñā* and *upāya* has to be effected through esoteric sexo-yogic practices. Esoteric elements like *mantras*, *dhāraṇīs*, *mudrās*, *maṇḍalas*, etc. play a vital role in *tāntrika* Buddhism. The sounds of the *mantras* were supposed to possess great spiritual powers, capable of protecting their reciters against all evil. The *dhāraṇīs* were practically the collection of *mantras*. *Dhāraṇī* signifies the inherent power of these mystic words for keeping up religious endeavours of a person. According to *tāntrika* Buddhists if a *mantra* rightly uttered, one can even get Buddhahood. The term *mudrā* signifies the postures of hands and figures of Buddha and Buddhist divinities, but in some *tāntrika* texts *mudrā* is termed as *prajñā*. The other term *maṇḍala* stands for mystic circle and its genesis may be traced back to the *bodhi-maṇḍala* or the circle around the famous tree under which Gautama attained *bodhi*. The institution of master (*guru*) and pupil (*śiṣya*) has been introduced to *tāntrika* Buddhism. Gradually a language of symbolism, intelligible only to the initiates developed. To the common man these words carried completely different meaning. This language was used intentionally not only for protecting the purity of yogic practices from the hands of the ignorant, but also for expressing the highest experience of the mind and body of the *sādhaka* concerned.

A large number of gods and goddesses are worshipped by the *tāntrika* Buddhists. A notable feature of this school is the introduction of a system of hierarchy of Buddhist divinities with Ādi Buddha at the apex.

Gradually *tāntrika* Buddhism adopted various cults and superstitions, beliefs and practices, breaking its relation with the original principles of Buddhism. The use of five *ma-kāra*s (i.e., the words beginning with the letter *ma*), such as *madya* (wine), *māṁsa* (meat), *matsya* (fish) *mudrā* (woman or physical gestures) and *maithuna* (sexual inter-course) became prominent for getting final perfection. The advocates of this school say that these five *ma*-elements are not actuated by the worldly desire, but they aim at the attainment of *bodhicitta*, the mental stage of supreme bliss.

Vajrayāna

This system is best expressive of the doctrinal and ritualistic characteristics of Tāntrism. In this system *vajra* connotes the unchangeable adamantine void-nature of the self and of the *dharma*s. Thus *Vajrayāna* is the way for the realisation of the *vajra*-nature or the chargeless and impenetrable void nature of the self and all entities. In course of time various heterogeneous elements got mixed up with it. These elements included, i.e., baneful *abhicāra* practice meant for causing harms to others (killing, enchanting etc.), the elaborate system of worshipping countless gods and goddesses of extensive pantheon, *mantras*, *gāthās* or verses, *maṇḍalas* or mystic circles *mudrās*, *pāramitās*, *haṭhayogas*, contemplative *Yoga* systems and sexo-yogic practices. Every item connected with Vajrayānic rituals and practices is preceded with *vajra*. For example some of the gods and goddesses of the *Vajrayāna* pantheon have names like Vajrarūpiṇī, Vajra-vilāsiṇī, Vajreśvarī etc.

The supreme Lord of this system is called Vajrasattva who represents Ultimate Reality, symbolising the non-dual state of *śūnyatā* (void) and *karuṇā* (compassion). He is Ādi Buddha, the possessor of five attributes or five kinds of knowledge and from these emerge five types of *dhyānas* or meditations which are symbolised by five *Dhyānī* Buddhas. Each of the *Dhyānī* Buddhas has his distinctive iconographic characteristics and consort as well as a corresponding Bodhisattva and a Mānuṣī Buddha and from each of them emanate a number of male and female deities.

The mode of worship and nature of meditation in *Vajrayāna* follow an eleborate paraphernalia, first the Lord supreme, then five *Dhyānī* Buddhas and their respective *Śakti's* are to be adored with offerings of flowers, incense, lamp etc. Then follow some other details including the devotee's confession of his sins before the Lord and taking refuge in the three jewels, Buddha, *Dharma* and *Saṁgha* and also taking vow for the production of *bodhicitta* for the well-being and salvation of all beings and to take the path followed by the *sugatas* and their followers, then the *sādhaka* is to meditate about the world as static and dynamic as all void and to place himself in the void. The last stage of the worship involves the meditation of the self as the Lord himself, with his accessory deities with *mantras*.[106]

Kālacakrayāna

The salient feature of this system of *tāntrika* Buddhism shows the clear difference from *Vajrayāna* in respect of the basic approach of esoteric *sādhanā* and hence *Kālacakrayāna* is recognised as a separate school of *tāntrika* Buddhism. The Primordial Lord of this school is called *Śrīkālacakra*, while *kāla* represents the ultimate perfect wisdom of *prajñā* which also means a state of *śūnyatā* or void nature, *cakra* signifies the cycle of world-process in the body of the Lord Supreme where remains the seed of world existence[107] and as such is identical with the principle of *upāya*. *Kālacakrayāna* differed from *Vajrayāna* in the introduction of some fearful and demonical gods with *śakti*s in the form of fiends (*ḍākini*s). These dreadful deities are very powerful and hold important position in this system. They believe that the whirl of Time (*kāla*) is the root behind all worldly miseries, decay and destruction and for the salvation, an elaborate system of Yogic practices is devised. It is conceived that the vital wind which is found in the human body causes Time with all its divisions and by controlling vital winds through yogic practices one can get out of the reach of whirl of Time and attain *bodhicitta*. So in this system astronomy and astrology get importance.

Sahajayāna

The protest against ritualism, *mantra*-charms etc. of *Vajrayāna* resulted in the birth of a new school called *Sahajayāna* about the eleventh and twelfth centuries AD in Bengal. It was popularised by some famous *siddha*s namely Saraha, Luipā, Kambala, Lalitavajra etc. According to this school of philosophy Reality and Appearance are not separated from each other, but are identical. This school gives importance to intuition and immotions. It looks man not only as an intellectual being, but also as an emotional one. The propagators of *Sahajayāna* are not inclined to destroy the sex passions or subdue any human instincts, but they try to sublimate them. To them any sort of suppression is harmful and hinders the realisation of Truth or the identify of Reality and Appearance.

The *caryāpada*s deal with *Sahajayāna* in the form of *dohā*s and devotional songs. The Sahajiyās say that *mahāsukha* signifies that the whole world is of the nature of *sahaja* — for *sahaja* is the quintessence (*svarūpa*) of all, this quintessence is *Nirvāṇa* to those who possess the perfectly pure *citta* (mind).[108] They give more importance on *guruvāda* or cult of preceptor than others. They also give much importance to human body, since without the body there is no possibility of the realisation of the great bliss. The main theme was to discover an individual's potentiality with the help of *guru*.

The views, the *tāntrika* Buddhism emanated from Hinduism and the *vice versa*, are not acceptable. *Tantra* is a system of *sādhanā*, involving religious and psycho-physiological exercises, emerged for the realisation of ultimate Truth, regardless of Hinduism and Buddhism. It was never a monopoly of either the Hindus or the Buddhists and both these religious sects developed Tantrism in their own ways and as they developed side by side, appearance of common elements in both the *tantra*-oriented system was but natural.

The origin of Tantrism can be looked at from different angles, acculturation of the peripheral areas though landgrants to the Buddhist monks and brāhmaṇas and the aboriginal background of the tāntric mother goddesses. Tantrism was the ultimate product of brāhmaṇised colonization of the tribal area through the process of landgrants. The confrontation between the brāhmaṇa beneficiaries and the tribal people created social and economic problems which were partly solved through Tantrism. On the one hand, the new religion welcomed in its ranks women, śūdras and the aborigines, on the other it recognised the existing social and feadual hierarchy. This was acceptable to all sections of people. It was a religious attempt at social reconciliation and integration.

Another social significance of the *Tantrayāna* is the *Dohākośa* of the Buddhist *siddhācārya*s. The *siddhācārya*s were itinerant bards and gave mystic answers to the existing social exploitation by the orthodox rigid social guardians. They refused to accept any dictum of institutionalised religion and their teachings found support among the tribal artisans like the *ḍoms* and *cāṇḍāla*s of the lower strata of society, living in the periphery of the brāhmaṇical social system. The language used by the *siddhācārya*s was *apabhraṁśa*, which was the language of the lower class of people. This also made this form of religion popular among the lower class of people.

The *tantra*s served an important social purpose by prescribing numerous rituals and remedies not only for the day-to-day diseases but also for snake-bites, mouse-bites, bites by poisonous insects and injuries supposed to be caused by ghosts. Remedies were laid down for the protection of cereals against being eaten by mice and vermins. Rites and occult practices were supposed to avert the adverse effects of diseases and planets.

The distinctive feature of the Buddhist *Tantrayāna* is ritual. Just as the case with other religions, Buddhists substituted a tangible, colourful and popular ritual for the old abstract meditations. The doctrine is to be acted out in tangible form instead of being simply understood.The ritual was useful in making a suitable impression on the inhabitants of the lands in possession of the temple. Through such rituals one could seek actively to realise supreme happiness and personal identity with the ultimate reality. Such ideals and attitudes offered to the rulers and the ruled, may have contributed significantly to social harmony and stability in a developing feudal order.[109]

Notes

1. *Taranatha* (tr.), D.P. Chattopadhyaya, p. 257.
2. *Ibid.*, p. 258.
3 G.S. Majumdar, *Buddhism in Ancient Bengal*, p. 31.
4. *MASI*, 55 (Paharpur, K.N. Dikshit).
5. *EI*, XVIII, p. 304.
6. *Ibid.*, p. 318.
7. D.P. Chattopadhyaya (tr.), *Taranatha's Buddhism*, p. 266.
8. *JAS*, XIII, 1971 pp. 201 ff.
9. *JASB*, *NS*, IV, p. 108.
10. *MASB*, V, p. 62.
11. *JASB*, N.S., 1908 IV, p. 105.
12. R.D. Banerji, *Palas of Bengal*, p. 75.
13. *JASB*, N.S. IV, p. 106.
14. *EI*, XXI, pp. 97-101.
15. D.P. Chattopadhyaya (tr), *Taranatha*, pp. 284-88.
16. G.S. Majumdar, *Buddhism in Ancient Bengal*, p. 43.
17. S.C. Das, *Journal of the Buddhist Text Society*, pp. 9-10.
18. Sandhyākaranandi, *The Rāmacarita*, IV, pp. 1-3.
19. Cunningham, ASI Reports III, p. 124, *JASB*, NS, IV, pp. 108-9.
20. D.P. Chattopadhya (tr.), *Taranatha*, pp. 313-14.
21. *JASB*, 1910, pp. 150-51.

22. *Ibid.*, 1900, pp. 66-73.
23. *JBORS*, XXI, 1935, pp. 42-43.
24. *EI*, XXVI, pp. 313 ff.
25. *EI*, XII, p. 136.
26. *JASB*, LXIX, p. 190.
27. *Ibid.*, p. 68.
28. *EI*, Vol XX, p. 61.
29. R.C. Majumdar (ed.), *The Struggle for Empire*, p. 415.
30. *Pag-sam-jon-Zang*, pp. lxxi, lxxv.
31. Taranatha (tr.) Banaras edition, pp. 200-1.
32. B.P. Sinha (ed.), *Comprehensive History of Bihar*, pp. 535-36.
33. *Supra*, p. 29.
34. Nicholas Roerich, *Blue Annals* II, p. 1031.
35. *Ibid.*, I, Calcutta, 1948, p. 243.
36. H.P. Shastri (ed.) (revised by R.G. Basak) p. 62.
37. *Asiatic Society Monthly Bulletin*, September, 1976.
38. D. Mitra, *Buddhist Monuments*, p. 244.
39. R.C. Majumdar, *History of Ancient Bengal*, p. 525.
40. D.K. Barua, *Viharas in Ancient India*, p. 180.
41. N.N. Dasgupta, *Bhāratavarśa*, 1341 B.S. pp. 962-70.
42. R.C. Majumdar, *History of Ancient Bengal*, p. 525.
43. *EI*, IV. p. 243, GL-9.
44. *JRAS*, 1909, p. 76.
45. R.C. Majumdar (ed.), *Age of Imperial Kanauj*, p. 269.
46. *Ibid.*
47. *Ibid.*, p. 270.
48. *Indian Antiquity*, Vol. XXI, p. 255.
49. *EI*, XVII, pp. 310-27.
50. *IA*, XV, p. 305.
51. *JVSP*, Vol. XV, p. 13.
52. R.D. Banerji, *Palas of Bengal*, p. 75.
53. *IA*, XIV, p. 139.
54. *JASB*, N.S. IV, p. 109.
55. *EI*, Vol. XV, pp. 1-8.
56. *JBORS* II, pp. 221-22.
57. *EI*, Vol. XIII, p. 167.
58. *EI*, Vol. XXVI, p. 247.

59. R.P. Chanda, *Memoirs of ASI No. 44*.
60. D. Chattopadhyaya (ed.), *Taranatha's History of Buddhism in India*, p. 144.
61. *EI*, Vol. XX, 21 ff.
62. T. Walters (III), *Yuen Chwang's Travels in India*, II, p.193.
63. Julien (tr.), *Hiuen Tsang's accounts*, I, p. 184.
64. R.L. Mitra, *Antiquities of Orissa*, II, p.59.
65. N.K. Sahu, *Buddhism in Orissa*, p. 50.
66. R.P. Chanda, *ASI Memoirs No. 44*, p. 6.
67. R.D. Banerji, *History of Orissa*, I, p. 137.
68. B. Mishra, *Dynasties of Medieval Orissa*, p. 93.
69. D. Chattopadhyaya (ed.), *Taranatha's History*, pp. 48-49.
70. *EI*, Vol. XV, pp. 363-64.
71. D. Mitra, *Buddhist Monuments*, pp. 227-28.
72. *EI*, Vol. XIX, pp. 263-64.
73. *Ibid.*
74. Walters II (tr.) p. 194.
75. *Ibid.*
76. *Ibid.*
77. *Ancient Geography of India*, p. 510.
78. *Proceedings of Asiatic Society of Bengal*, December, 1982.
79. B. Mishra, *Orissa under the Bhauma Kings*, p. 40.
80. K.C. Panigrahi, *History of Orissa*, p. 455.
81. D. Mitra, *Bronzes from Achutarājpur*, p. 53.
82. D. Mitra, *Buddhist Monuments*, p. 225.
83. N.K. Sahu, *Buddhism in Orissa*, p. 215.
84. R.D. Banerji, *History of Orissa* I, p. 145.
85. D. Mitra, *Buddhist monuments*, p. 232.
86. *EI*, XV (1919-20) p.5.
87. D.P. Chattopadhyaya (ed.), *Lama Taranatha's History of Buddhism in India*.
88. *EI*, XV (1919-20) p. 5.
89. *JBORS*, II, IV, 1916, p. 4.
90. B. Das, *The Bhaumakaras and Their times*, p. 145.
91. *EI*, Vol. XV, (1919-20), p. 1.
92. *Ibid.*, XXIX (1951-52), p. 210.
93. *Ibid.*, XXVI, (1941-42) pp. 247-48.
94. *Ibid.*, XXVIII, (1949-50), p. 214.
95. *Ibid.*, XIII, (1915-16), p. 167.

96. *Ibid.*, XXVIII, pp. 211-16.
97. *Ibid.*
98. *Ibid.*, XXVIII, p. 180.
99. P. Mukherji, *History of Medieval Vaishnavism in Orissa*, pp. 20-21.
100. *JBORS*, Vol. XVI, pp. 69-83.
101. *Ibid.*, II, 88 pp. 419 ff.
102. *EI*, Vol. XXIX, pp. 210 ff.
103. *JBORS*, Vol. II, pp. 419-27.
104. K.C. Panigrahi, *Archaeological Remains at Bhubneswar*, pp. 32-33.
105. Among these *Guhyasamāja tantra* has been edited by Biswanath Banerji.
106. *TB*, pp. 83-85 (*Introduction to Tāntric Buddhism* by S.B. Dasgupta) Calcutta, 1950.
107. *Sekoddesa-tika* (ed. by Marie E. Carelli) taken from *Buddhism in Ancient Bengal* by Gayatri Sen Majumdar.
108. *Hevajra-tantra*, ASB, MS. No 11317, folio 36B. (taken from *Buddhism in Ancient Bengal* by G.S. Majumdar).
109. Sharma, R.S. (ed.), *Indian Society, Historical Probings*, p. 174.

4

Society in Bengal and Orissa

SOCIETY UNDER THE PĀLAS OF BENGAL

People

We find two elements in the people of Bengal from the ethnological point of view. They are (i) the primitive tribes like the Kols, Sabaras, Pulindas, Hāḍi, Ḍom, Cāṇḍāla and Mlecchas, and (ii) others consisting of the higher classes of people which come within the framework of the caste system. The first group of people are descendants of the earliest inhabitants of Bengal and the majority, if not the whole of them, were probably descended from the non-Āryan people of the Ṛgvedic age, referred to as Niṣādas in the Vedic literature. They were submerged by new waves of people with a high culture and civilization.

There is little doubt about the coming of Āryans into Bengal, in an increasing number, from an early period, either in the wake of military attacks or for more peaceful pursuits. The Āryans included followers of different religious sects Brāhmaṇical, Buddhist and Jaina. The pace of immigration was quickened by the establishment of the political power of the Guptas in Bengal. Gupta rule in Bengal also gave an ascendancy to the orthodox followers of Brāhmaṇical religion.

The inscriptions of the Gupta period, which for the first time, give us a definite knowledge about the religion and society of Bengal, refer to orthodox brāhmaṇas performing *smārta* and *śrauta* rites (rituals according to *Smṛti* and *Śruti* texts respectively) and Purāṇic worship all over Bengal. These inscriptions show the complete domination of Āryan influence in all classes of society, both urban and rural. Therefore, as available evidence goes, we may regard that the essential features of Āryan society was present in Bengal as early as the fifth century AD. From the literary and epigraphic records we can conclude that the social developement in Bengal took place more or less on the same lines as in the rest of Northern India.

It is significant to note that even though the Pālas were Buddhists, the orthodox system of caste was upheld, as an ideal by the kings. From the epigraphic records we came to know that Dharmapāla, though a follower of Buddhism, maintained the rules of castes and religious orders in strict conformity to the holy scriptures. This example shows that the personal religious belief of the ruler did not influence the policy of the state, which was based on the time-honoured precepts and conventions.

The most characteristic feature of the society was the existence of innumerable castes and sub-castes. It is a well-known fact that the division of people into four *varṇa*s, viz. br āhmaṇas, kṣatriyas, vaiśyas and śūdras, was merely a theory, except perhaps in the most ancient period. Numerous castes and sub-castes had been evolved by the time Āryan culture entered Bengal. It was possible due to the developement of different arts, crafts and professions and partly also due to the racial, tribal and religious factors.[1]

The authors of *Dharma-Śāstra*s and *Smṛti*s (Brāhmaṇical Scriptures dealing with rituals) considered the *Veda*s as infallible and thereafter they laboured hard to maintain the four *varṇa* system. Hence they started with the theory that the numerous castes, actually existing, arose from the unions of males and females belonging to *varṇa*s, differing from their own. This is popularly known as *varṇa-saṅkara* (mixed caste). The *Bṛhad-dharma Purāṇa*[2] of the twelfth century AD reflects the peculiar social conditions in Bengal. It authorises the brāhmaṇas to eat fish and meat and divides the non-brāhmaṇic population into thirtysix castes, all described as śūdras. These are characteristic features of Bengal society. The *Bṛhad-dharma Purāṇa* describes how King Veṇa, bent upon violating the rules of *varṇāśrama* (caste system prescribed by *Dharmasūtras*), deliberately created a number of mixed castes by forcing the unions of males and females belonging to different castes, which included not only the original four castes, but also the mixed castes resulting from their union. It differs from the general body of the *Smṛtis* in deriving the mixed castes not from marriage of males and females of different castes, but from their indiscriminate union at the bidding of or under the compulsion, exercised by the king. Although Veṇa is represented as an opponent to orthodox Brāhmaṇical cults in epics, *Smṛtis* and *Purāṇas*, no other text ascribes to him the origin of mixed castes as we find in the *Brhad-dharma Purāṇa*.

The castes that arose out of these promiscuous unions are classified as *uttama*, *madhyama* and *adhama saṅkaras*, all having the status of śūdra.[3]

I. *Uttama (High) Saṅkaras*

(i) The Karanas, who were good scribes and efficient in office work.

(ii) The Ambashthas called Vaidyas, who studied *Ayurveda* and manufactured medicines.

(iii) The Ugras who practised military arts.

(iv) The Māgodha who did the work of court bard and carrier of messages.

(v) *Tantravāya* — the weaver.

(vi) *Gandhika-vaṇik* — dealer in spices etc.

(vii) *Nāpita* — the barber

(viii) *Gopa* — the writer

(ix) *Karmakāra* — the blacksmith

(x) *Taulika* — who dealt with betelnut

(xi) *Kumbhakāra* — the potter

(xii) *Kaṁsākāra* — the brazier

(xiii) *Sānkhika* — conch-shell worker

(xiv) *Dāsa* — cultivator
(xv) *Vārajīvī* — betelvine growers
(xvi) *Modaka* — sweetmeat maker
(xvii) *Mālākāra* — florist

II. *Madhyama (Intermediate) Saṅkaras*

(i) *Takṣan* — carpenter
(ii) *Rajaka* — washerman
(iii) *Svarṇakāra* — goldsmith
(iv) *Svarṇavaṇik* — trader in bullion
(v) *Ābhira* — cowherd or milkman
(vi) *Tailakāraka* — oilman
(vii) *Dhivara* — fisherman
(viii) *Saundika* — vintmen
(ix) *Naṭa* — dancer, acrobat or juggler
(x) *Sāvāka* or *Sāvāra* — sarak
(xi) *Sekhara*
(xii) *Jālika* — fisherman

III. *Adhama (Low) Saṅkaras or Antyajas,* outside the pale of caste

(i) *Malagrahi* — mal caste?
(ii) *Kudava* — boatman?
(iii) *Cāṇḍāla*
(iv) *Varuda* — baori?
(v) *Takṣa* — carpenter?
(vi) *Carmakāra* — leather worker
(vii) *Ghantajīvī* — patni caste
(viii) *Dolā vāhi* — palanquin-bearer
(ix) *Malla* — modern māla?

The above division into three classes is said to be based on a definite principle viz. (1) those whose father and mother both belong to the four primitive castes are regarded as class I, (2) those whose mothers alone belong to one of these primitive castes but fathers belong to class I form class II, (3) those whose father and mother both belong to any mixed caste are relegated to class III.

The *śrotriya* brāhmaṇas are permitted to function as priests only of the twenty mixed castes belonging to class I (mentioned above). The priests of the other castes are said to be degraded brāhmaṇas, who attain the status of the castes they serve.

The gradual disappearance of a distinct kṣatriya caste, the progressive assimilation of the vaiśya with the śūdra and the division of the śūdra into *sat* and *asat* (higher and lower) were the main features of this period.

As regards the status of the different castes, the Karanas and the Ambasthas are given the positions of pre-eminence. The Ambasthas are equated with the Vaidyas and the Karanas were forerunners of the Kāyasthas.

A distinctive feature of this period was the predominance of the Kāyasthas and Vaidyas among the other castes except brāhmaṇas. Such castes as *saṁkhakāra, dāsa* (cultivator), *tantuvāya, modaka, karmakāra* and *suvarṇa-vaṇik* are well-known in Bengal, but are not generally met with in other parts of India.

At various times, the relative status, the number and designation of different castes must have varied. The reference to the Pāla kings as having maintained the system of caste, indirectly implies, the right and duty of the royal authority to maintain the *status quo* in the sphere of social life.

Although arts, crafts and professions were generally hereditary and the different castes normally followed the vocations, assigned to them, it is now generally accepted that there was never any absolute rigidity or exclusiveness in actual practice which is corroborated from the epigraphic and literary sources found from Bengal. We have evidence of brāhmaṇas becoming soldiers, rulers, adminstrators and followers of other vocations. The Karanas practised medicine and military arts, the Vaidyas became ministers and *dāsa*s served as officials and court poets.[4]

Although marriage among members of the same caste was the ordinary rule, intermarriage between the male of the higher and the female of the lower caste was regarded as valid, down to the last days of the Hindu period.[5] The śūdra wife of the upper caste was being subjected to special disabilities but the validity of her marriage and her right to maintenance were not questioned.

In this period, restrictions about food and drink between different castes were not much rigid as it became during the nineteenth century AD. The restrictions about drink affected the brāhmaṇas alone and only in respect of śūdras and a few low castes, definitely specified. The brāhmaṇas did not lose caste by taking food from other castes and only penances were prescribed for even the worst transgression, such as taking food from a *cāṇḍāla*.

The contemporary sources indicate that gradually inter-dining and inter-marriage was not permitted between brāhmaṇa and low caste. But soon it came to be regarded as marks of aristocracy and were extended to other castes.

The *Bṛhad-dharma Purāṇa* regards śūdras as one of the most notable castes of Bengal, most probably due to the predominance of Buddhism and Tāntric-Śāktism in Bengal since the eighth century AD.

We have no reliable reference to any kṣatriya or vaiśya family in Bengal. This does not mean that there was no kṣatriya or vaiśya caste in Bengal. The Senas, who called themselves kṣatriyas, were immigrants from Karnāṭa and the Pālas are not designated as kṣatriyas. Thus our knowledge about these two castes in Bengal is only restricted to the reference to kṣatriya and vaiśyas on the writings of Bhavadeva Bhaṭṭa and other writers on sacred laws of this period.

Brāhmaṇas

The settlement of brāhmaṇas in Bengal, hailing from Latā (Gujarat), Madhyadeśa (central India), such localities as Krodanchi (Kolāncha). Tarakāri (Śrāvastī), Chandavāra (Etāwā in U.P.) etc., is corroborated from the contemporary inscriptions. It is a fact that most of the brāhmaṇas had been brought to Bengal during this period by the royal dynasties of Bengal, as that was the common practice in most parts of India.

These brāhmaṇas were ultimately settled in Bengal and were granted villages for maintenance. They derived their surnames (*gāmī*) from these villages, and were the forefathers of the brāhmaṇa community except the *Vaidikas*, who came at a later period. The *Saptaśatīs*, consisting of the remnants of the original brāhmaṇas were degraded to a lower rank and gradually disappeared without leaving any trace. In course of time the brāhmaṇas in Bengal were divided into various sub-castes or branches such as *raḍhiya, varendra, vaidika,* and *śaktidvīpī*, according to the area of their domicile or the family of their ancestors.

The *varendra* and *rāḍhiya* brāhmaṇas lived in Varendra and Rāḍhā respectively. They were classified in several grades according to personal qualifications. These grades were revised from time to time. We see more than hundred of such divisions before the fifeenth century AD when they became hereditary.

The *vaidika* brāhmaṇas who came from upper India, came to be known as *pāścātya* (western) and those came from south India and Utkala (Orissa), came to be known as *dakṣiṇātya* (southern). Halāyudha[6] observes in his *Brāhmaṇa-Sarvasva* that the *rāḍhiya* and *varendra* brāhmaṇas have no knowledge of the Vedic texts which are studied only by the Utkalas and the *Pāścātyas*.

The performance of religious rites, serving as priests and studying and teaching of *Vedas* and other sacred texts were some of the main functions of the brāhmaṇas. Apart from sacrificial fees, donations, large or small, were made to the brāhmaṇas by kings and private persons, as such gifts were considered to confer *puṇya* (spiritual merits) on the donors.

Besides the above-mentioned functions, the brāhmaṇas also followed many other vocations both high and low. Two important brāhmaṇa families, renowned for their scholarship and knowledge of sacred Vedic rites and sacrifices, served the Pāla and Varman kings as counsellors and generals maintaining at the same time their high position in the Brāhmaṇical society. The brāhmaṇas who taught the śūdras and officiated at their sacrificial rites were regarded as degraded brāhmaṇas. This resulted in the creation of new classes of brāhmaṇas in Bengal.

Karana-Kāyastha

From the high offices and position occupied by the Karanas during this period, it appears that this caste occupied a very important position only next to the brāhmaṇas in Bengal. The caste Karana-Kāyastha is referred to in the Ganaighar CP.[7] The author of *Śabda-Pradīpa*, a text on medicine, belonging to a Karana family says that he and his forefathers served as court physician under Rāmapāla and Govindacandra of Bengal.[8] Sandhyākara Nandi, the author of *Rāmacarita*, describes his father as the foremost amongst the Karanas and served as Minister of peace and war.[9] It seems that the Karanas gradually merged themselves into the Kāyastha caste after twelfth century AD and these two castes were ultimately amalgamated.

The Tibetan work *Pag-sam-jon-zang* mentions Dangadāsa, a writer during the period of Dharmapāla as a Kāyastha.[10] Kāyasthas were recongnised as a caste in Bengal by the tenth century AD.[11]

Vaidya-Ambastha

The term *vaidya*, denoted to the physician was an important profession at that time. It is not known when this professional group was developed into a caste. The earliest reference to Vaidya, as a distinct social group, occurs in three south Indian inscriptions of the eighth century AD.[12] The members of this group occupied very high positions in state and society. But there is no definite reference to Vaidya as a caste in Bengal before the twelfth century AD. *Dharmasūtras* describe the Ambastha caste as a mixed caste, born of a brāhmaṇa father and vaiśya mother. Manu prescribes the art of healing as his vocation.[13] It seems that the Vaidya was an offshoot of the Ambastha caste.

Low Castes

The early *caryā-padas* (poems dealing with Buddhism) of Bengal refer to ḍoma, *caṇḍāla* and *savara*, as the lowest castes in the society. The ḍomas lived outside the town and were regarded as untouchables. They built baskets and looms (*tant*). The *savaras* lived in hills. The *cāṇḍālas* or *antyajas* were said to have occasionally abducted married women from their homes. The *antyaja* is defined as a group of seven low castes viz. *rajaka* (washerman), *Carmakāra* (leatherman), *naṭa* (actor), *kaivarta* (fisherman), *meda* and *bhilla* (tribals).[14]

Socio-Religious Rites, Ceremonies and Festivals

From the writings of Bhaṭṭa Bhavadeva, Jimutavāhana, Aniruddha Bhaṭṭa, Vallālasena and others we get informations about the Brāhmaṇical society of Bengal during the eleventh and twelfth century AD. From these sources we come to know that the life of the orthodox Hindus particularly the brāhmaṇas, was characterised by the various purificatory rites and ceremonies, concerning almost every stage of a man's life, starting from conception in the mother's womb to death or even beyond it. Some of these were *Garbhādhāna* (ceremony of impregnation), *Jāta-karman* (birth ceremony), *Nāmakaraṇa* (ceremony of naming the child), *Annaprāsana* (ceremony of giving solid food to the child for the first time), *Upanayana* (sacred thread investing ceremony) and *Vivāha* (marriage ceremony). In all these ceremonies the domestic fire was first to be consecrated and *homas* (oblation given to fire) were to be performed with the citation of relevant Vedic *mantras*.

Marriage

Sapiṇḍa, sagotra and *samāna-pravara* (regarding relationship between the bride and bridegroom) were given much importance in the matters of marriage. No marriage was permitted if the bride was within the fifth generation on the mother's side of the bridegroom or within the seventh generation on his father's side or if the bride and bridegroom of the same *gotra* or of the same *pravara*. Monogamy was the ideal, though sometimes people had more than one wife. This could be possible only when the person, who wanted to have a second wife, had to gratify the first one with sufficient wealth in order to have her assent. Whatever might be the number of the wives of a person, first *savarṇa* (of the same caste) wife enjoyed the highest position in social and religious functions. *Brāhma*, *daiva*, *arśa*, *prājāpatya*, *asura*, *gandharva*, *rākṣasa* and *paiśāca* were some of the forms of marriage prevalent in Bengal like other parts of India. *Brāhma* form of marriage was the most popular among brāhmaṇas. Generally marriage ceremony was accompanied by various festivities and amusements. People generally were in favour of early marriage of girls.

Festivals

The festivals related to the worship of Durgā, Gaṇeśa, Sarasvatī, Indra, Sūrya, Mānasa, the spring festival *Holī*, the *Sukha-rātri-vrata*, the *Dyuta pratipad* (playing chess), the *Pāśāna Caturdaśī* were some of the festivities enjoyed by the people of Bengal. These festivals provided oppertunities to people to come into close and intimate touch with one another and also made the family and social life highly enjoyable.

Life of the People

The sources for obtaining information about the life of people of Bengal, in the period of our study, are foreign accounts, sculptures, literature and inscriptions. But the datas provided by these sources are not adequate to get a clear picture of the social life in Bengal.

The Chinese traveller Hiuen-Tsang[15] has recorded that the people of Samataṭa were hardy by nature and those of Tāmralipti, both hardy and brave. An excessive love of learning and earnest application to it characterised the people of Puṇḍravardhana, Samataṭa and Karna-suvarna. Kṣemendra, in his satirical poem *Dasopadeśa,*[16] mentioned that the people of Bengal were not good in their behaviour. The Brāhmaṇical writers of Bengal always insisted on a high moral standard of people and encouraged a culture of all kinds of virtue such as truth, charity, purity, kindness and continence.

Position of Women

Women of ancient Bengal were educated. From the love letters written by women, referred by Dhoyi, in his *Pavanadūta*, (the wind-messenger) it is clear that many women were literate.[17] From, Dhoyi's description of the women of Vijayapura, the capital of Lakṣmaṇa Sena, it is known that the *purdāh* (veil) system was not much in vogue.[18] It is very interesting to find that the great Bengal jurist Jimutavāhana asserts the right of a widow to inherit her husband's entire property in the absence of any male issue. He further says, that the widow shall have no right to sale, mortgage or gift of the property and her enjoyment should be consistent with the life of a chaste widow, solely devoted to the memory of her husband. She should live in her husband's family and abstain from luxury. Polygamy was prevalent in this period all over India. So Bengal cannot be an exception. Married women sometimes helped their husbands by earning money through spinning or weaving. The widows were often looked upon as inauspicious and were very rarely allowed to take part in the different rites and ceremonies. Though the widows seem to have been encouraged by the people to immolate themselves in the funeral pyres of their husbands[19] (known as *satī* sacrifice), there were very rare cases of *satī* during the period of our research.

Food and Drink

The chief articles of diet were rice, fish, meat, fruits, vegetables and milk. In other parts of India the brāhmaṇas usually did not take fish and meat, but in Bengal the practice was very common. But the brāhmaṇas were not allowed to take those fishes which had ugly forms or heads like snakes or lived in holes.[20] Though the people were asked to avoid rotton fish, some of them took dried fish.[21] In no case taking of raw or dried meat was permitted.[22] Among vegetables mushrooms, onions, garlics etc. were to be avoided.[23]

Betels were commonly eaten by the people of Bengal. It was taken with *kapūra* (camphor).

Though Bhavadeva,[24] in his book *Prāyaścitta Prakaraṇa*, vehemently opposed the taking of intoxicating drink, people were taking country made liquor, made by distillation of rice, molasses, flour and honey.

Dress and Ornaments

From the sculptures of Pahārapur, it is noticed that men of that time wore *dhotī*, generally shorter and narrower than that worn by the Bengalis of the present-day.

The usual mode of wearing the *dhotī* was different from the present fashionable mode. The women wore *sārīs* in the same way as the males wore, but they were much longer and reached the ankle. The *sārīs* like the *dhotī*, never covered the upper part of the body which generally remained exposed, though sometimes it was partially covered by a long narrow scarf called *uttarīya* or *oḍhnī*. In addition, the women covered the upper part of their body by *colī* (blouse). The *sārīs* and *dhotīs* were embroidered with various designs.

The dancing girls wore close fitting *pyjāmā* (loose trousers type), reaching up to the ankle and a long *oḍhnā* (long scarf).

The ornaments both for men and women were almost same. The sculptures of couple in Pahārpur relief have each large ear-pendants, two lines of necklaces, armlets, bracelets, anklets etc. Neither men nor women used any covering for the head, though the Pahārpur sculptures show that they elaborately dressed their hair.

Except warriors, no figure in Pahārpur sculptures, is represented with any footwear, which make us believe that it was probably not in common use at that time.

The custom of married women marking their forehead with vermilion, is marked from the sculptures. The women also reddened their lower lips with vermilion, used saffron as a cosmetic and painted their feet with lac.[25]

Games and Past times

Dice and chess seem to be the most favourable indoor games during that period. The *Caryāpadas*[26] described in details about the game of chess. The *Caryāpadas* also refer to music, both vocal and instrumental, dancing and theatrical performances. Music and dancing were considered, as high classes of art, by both men and women. *Devadāsīs* (temple dancers) in the temples strictly followed the directions about dance and music given in the *Nāṭyasūtra* of Bharata and other texts on this subject.

Among outdoor past times of women, may be mentioned gardening and watersports.[27] Men favoured wrestling and acrobatics. This fact is known from the Pahārapur plates.[28]

Luxury and Morality

Though Bengal was primarily a rural country, still it had a number of towns and commercial centres, which were places of wealth and luxury. The description of Rāmāvati[29] and the Vijayapura,[30] the capital cities of the Pālas and Senas, by two contemporary poets, gives us a vivid picture of the wealthy cities of ancient Bengal. These towns contained wide roads and symmetrical rows of palatical buildings, towering high and surmounted by golden pitchers on the top. The temples, monasteries, public parks and large tanks, bordered by tall palm trees, added to the beauty and amenities of town life.

Both literary and epigraphic evidences testify to the immorality and sensual excess in early medieval Bengal. *Kāmasūtra* and Dhoyi's *Pavanadūta* have described about this aspect in detail. The language of Dhoyi seems to imply that these were not merely tolerated but regarded as part of normal social life.

The low morality standard was responsible for the growth of certain evil customs. The general practice of keeping female slaves, referred to by Jimutavāhana, was one of the examples of the moral degradation of the people. Another evil result of immorality was the system of dedicating young girls (*devadāsīs*) for service in the temples. Whatever might have been the primary nature and objective of the '*devadāsī* system' in India, there is no doubt of its degradation in Bengal, towards the close of the twelfth century AD.

The reasons for this moral degradation are many. One of the reasons is the inevitable consequence of the Tāntric doctrines and the religious tenets and practices of the last phase of both Brāhmaṇical and Buddhist religions in the eleventh and twelfth centuries AD. The literature of this period and the religious texts and practices of the later phases of both Hinduism and Buddhism occasionally betray a degradation in ideas of decency and sexual morality which could not but seriously affect the healthy development of moral and social life.[31]

Education and Learning

This period saw a great development of literature and learning. Both Brāhmaṇical and Buddhistic Sanskrit literature flourished in Bengal during this period. Some of the epigraphic records give us examples of rich state of literary activities of that period.

Nārāyāṇapāla's Bādāl pillar inscription[32] gives us a detailed account of the scholarly pursuit of one of the minister families of the Pāla kings, which was famous for the knowledge of Vedic literature. In this family Darbhapani, who worked under Devapāla as a minister, and his grandson Kedāramiśra are said to have mastered in four *Vedas*. The colophon to the *Hari-carita Kāvya* of Chaturbhuja[33] mentions that the Varendra brāhmaṇas of the time of Dharmapāla were experts in *Śruti*, *Smṛti*, *Purāṇa*, *Vyākaraṇa* and *Kāvya*.

But unfortunately the epigraphic indications of cultural activity, are not fully borne out by the actual literary remains of this period. Only we get some Buddhist Tāntric writings belonging to this period.

One of the most important literary works of this period, in which we find the origin of Bengali language, is the *Ramacarita* of Sandhyākara Nandi.[34] It belongs to the category of historical *Kāvya*. It contained 220 verses in which the story of *Rāmāyāṇa* as well as the history of Rāmapāla of the Pāla dynasty were described. It appears probable that the work was completed in the reign of Madanapāla, son of Rāmapāla.

The epigraphic records of this period tell us about the Vedic and philosophical studies in Bengal, but no early work on Vedic as well as Philosophical literature has survived. The only philosophical work of this period was the *Nyāya-kandali* commentary of Śrīdhara Bhaṭṭa on Praśastapāda's *Padārtha-dharma-saṁgraha Bhāṣya* on the *Vaiśeṣika-sūtra*.

Literatures on medical profession also were created during this period. One example is a glossary of medical botany named *Śabda-pradīpa*, written by Sureśvara or Surapāla.

We know about two important Bengal writers on *Dharmaśāstras*, named Bhavadeva and Aniruddha. The *praśasti* of Bhavadeva and his family, composed by Bhavadeva's friend Vācaspati-Kavi, consists of thirty-three elegantly written verses.[35]

A fragment of Bhavadeva's work on *Mīmāṁsā* philosophy of Kumārila Bhaṭṭa named *Tautātita-mata-tilaka* is available to us. Bhavadeva belonged to the twelfth century AD.[36]

Another important *Dharmaśāstra* authority of this period in Bengal was Jimutavāhana. The date of Jimutavāhana is still a matter of controversy. Manmohan Chakravarti,[37] after analysing astronomical as well as literary evidences, fixed his date in the beginning of the twelfth century AD. Jimutavāhana's three works were very famous. The most important one is his *Dayābhāga*,[38] which deals with the Hindu Law of inheritance, partition, and *strīdhana* (women wealth) in Bengal. His other work *Vyavahāra-mātrikā*[39] is on judicial procedure. His third work *Kāla-viveka*[40] deals on time like season, month, day and hour for the performance of religious duties and ceremonies.

We find a large number of Buddhist literary works during this period. Though the Sanskrit versions of these works are mostly lost, we have Tibetan translations. Due to the patronage given by the Buddhist Pāla kings, the Buddhist writers of this period could contribute all such things to us. The works deal with different *yāna*s or *tantra*s. They teach esoteric doctrines, rites and practices in a highly symbolic language. It was during this period that the monasteries-cum-academic institutions like Nālandā, Vikramaśilā, Jagaddala and Somapuri became famous centres of Buddhist learning with which the composition and translation of many of these Tāntric works are associated. Great Buddhist scholars like Candragomin, Śāntideva, Śānti (or Śānta)rakṣita, Jetāri, Dipāṅkara Śrījñāna, and Jñānaśrīmitra belonged to this period and created many works concerning religion, grammar, philosophy, logic etc.

Thus the period from eighth to twelfth century in Bengal witnessed a great development of education and learning. Secular subjects were also taught during this period. India, particularly Bengal, maintained a cultural relationship with many foreign countries like Nepal, Tibet and China due to the Buddhist educational centres in different parts of Bengal.

SOCIETY UNDER THE BHAUMAKARAS OF ORISSA

Caste system has been the most important feature of the Indian social life since very early times. From the epigraphic records of the Bhaumakaras it appears that the division of society into four castes prevailed during this time in Orissa. But this fourfold *varṇa* system no longer remained a functional reality. It remained as a model in an ideal typical sense. Land-grants accompanied by the transfer of various rights to both secular and religious donees and the process of sub-infeudation created new production relations in this period. The process of feudalisation affected the pattern of social stratification more than any other factor like religion. Unequal distribution of land and power on a large scale affected the traditional *varṇa* system by the creation of new social groups.

By this time Buddhism had entered every nook and corner of Orissa. Side by side the brāhmaṇas continued to pour into Orissa from different parts of northern India. Several ruling dynasties of this period including the Bhaumakaras followed the practice of giving large scale land-grants to the brāhmaṇas and to other religious communities. This process helped in the increase of food production and in rural expansion.

Though the early Bhaumakara kings were Buddhists, they tried to enforce *varṇāśramadharma*, a Brāhmaṇic concept of caste system. In the Neulpur charter of Bhauma king Śubhakara I, it is mentioned that the first king of the Bhaumakara dynasty king Kṣemaṅkara put *varṇa*s in their proper places.[41] Similarly the Terundia charter of the Bhaumakara King Śubhakara II points out that the donor established the *varṇāśrama* order in its golden age purity in strict accordances with the scriptures.[42] There were constant efforts from the Bhauma kings to curb *varṇa-saṅkara* (mixed castes) and uphold *varṇāśramadharma*. It was felt necessary by the kings, as the castes ignored their respective duties. Besides this, in order to get legitimacy from the brāhmaṇas this *varṇāśramadharma* had to be implemented by the kings.

This observation was valid in Bengal also. It is significant to note that the Buddhist faith (which opposed caste-system) of the rulers of Orissa and Bengal did not stop in their way of maintaining the caste system in society. The protection of the established order of society was an important aspect of state craft and maintenance of the social order, based on caste, was the most important function of the Head of the state.

Brāhmaṇas

There were numerous castes and sub-castes in Orissa during this period. The records do not provide information about the position of different castes. But from other sources it is known that the brāhmaṇas, like in other parts of India, occupied the highest position in the social hierarchy. The brāhmaṇas enjoyed great honour in society for their pious life and devotion to the studies of the *Vedas*. The *Dharmaśāstras* praise them and say that they are the agents of God on earth. Though the *Matsya Purāṇa*[43] declared Oḍra to be a land of degraded brāhmaṇas, still in this period we find the flow of brāhmaṇas from Madhyadeśa, Śrāvastī etc. We have to consider certain factors in order to know the reasons for their influx. It was the time when the Northern empires were disintegrating and the brāhmaṇas were in search of stable countries for their survival. They found Orissa to be an ideal place for clientele. Another reason for the influx was the growing competition among the brāhmaṇas in other parts of India which led them seek outlet in Orissa which offered them status and position under royal patronage.

After firmly settled in Orissa the brāhmaṇas tried to preach *varṇa* ideology in order to acculturate the tribals. By the tenth century AD the position of brāhmaṇas in Orissa was elevated to such a height that they were included in one of the five major sections of the brāhmaṇas in North India.[44] The *Utkal-khaṇḍa* of *Skanda Purāna* (the section dealing with Orissa) says that brāhmaṇa is the guru of all *varṇas*. We find there was proliferation among brāhmaṇas due to many factors such as the place of migration, differences in *gotra*, *parvara*, *cāranas* and *sakhās*, the levels of learning and branches of specialization and the absorption of tribal priests.

Uneven distribution of landgrants created a hierarchy within the brāhmaṇa caste. Those who occupied administrative and military posts must have had high social status among brāhmaṇas. Epigraphic sources state the various professions practised by the brāhmaṇas. Besides studying and teaching *Vedas*, the brāhmaṇas were associated with astrology. The socio-economic compulsions led to a sizeable section of the brāhmaṇas to take to priestly activities in the temples and villages. Those brāhmaṇas who commercialised their priestly services would have stood degraded in the eyes of the *śāsana* brāhmaṇas (very high grade brāhmaṇa). It is significant to note that the brāhmaṇas of this period followed many vocations, both religious and secular.

Kṣatriya

The word kṣatriya has not been mentioned by any inscriptions of this period in Orissa. We have references to kṣatriya caste in the *Skanda Purāṇa* (*Utkala Khaṇḍa*)[45] and also in the records of Hieun-Tsang.[46] The references to *rānakas*, *mahārājās* and *mahāsāmantas* etc. in several Bhauma epigraphic records indicate the existence of the kṣatriya caste in Orissan society. The fact that the Bhauma kings established matrimonical relations with prominent kṣatriya families outside Orissa indicates the existence of kṣatriyas in Orissa.

The origin and the caste of the Bhaumakara kings have been the subject of much controversy. According to Prof. R.D. Banerji,[47] the Bhaumakaras were descended from the non-Āryan *Asuras* of Kāmarūpa. But the *praśasti* of the grant of Daṇḍī Mahādevī, one of the rulers of the Bhaumakara dynasty, has led H. Pandey[48] to think that the Bhaumas belonged to the Lunar race of the kṣatriyas.

The situation seems to have changed a great deal as the process of state formation gained momentum. The ruling families, in order to achieve territorial expansion and sovereign power, tried to attain the status of kṣatriya. To legitimatise their position they started the process of brāhmaṇisation and had matrimonial contacts with nobles of outside powers. The ruling chiefs proclaimed themselves as kṣatriyas by tracing their lineage to a mythical ancestry and by adopting various *gotras*, which was given legitimacy by the brāhmaṇas. The use of epithets by the king like *parameśvara*, *paramabhaṭṭāraka*, *paramopāsaka* etc. show that the rulers tried to connect themselves with divinity.

Training in military science and art of warfare was very essential for the kṣatriya princes of this period, before taking the reigns of administration of a kingdom. There were instances of the kings personally commanding the army in the battlefield and displaying great skill. The kings were not only expert in the use of arms but also experts in different branches of learning. The Tālcher plate of Śivakara described Śubhakara IV as deeply conversant with the *śāstras*.

The non-ruling kṣatriyas took civil and military services. Sometimes they also followed other peaceful vocations. The kṣatriyas occupied an important position in the social hierarchy and though their position was next to the brāhmaṇas, in reality they enjoyed a position same as the brāhmaṇas.

Kāyasthas-Karanas

The inscriptions of Orissa prior to the tenth century AD do not indicate the existence of the Kāyastha as a caste. In the inscriptions of the periods in the tenth century and onwards, we find the mention of terms like *mahākāyas*, the *kāyastha*, *karana* etc.

As to the origin of the Kāyastha or Karana caste, R.S. Sharma,[49] opines that constant transfer of land and land revenue made by the princes to various donees must have led to the rise of a class of scribes, drawn from the literate members of the higher *varṇas*, who in course of time came to be known as Kāyasthas or Karanas.

The Kāyasthas were entrusted with high responsible duties of the ministers and high royal executives. Some Kāyasthas also served in the army in Orissa. It is interesting to note that while in many parts of North India, the Kāyasthas worked as scribes and wrote charters and documents, in Orissa we find only a few instances of this type.

Vaiśyas

The *Utkala Khaṇḍa* of the *Skanda Purāṇa*, while referring to the Puruṣottamakṣetra (Orissa as land of Lord Jagannāth), says that agriculture, trade and cattle rearing were the occupations of the vaiśyas. No inscription of the Bhauma mentions about the vaiśyas. According to eminent historian S. Jaiswal, the vaiśya *varṇa* did not emerge in Orissa during the early medieval period.[50] In the course of acculturation and peasantization, the land owning peasantry must have got themselves distinguished from the culturally backward tribes. They were the ones who must have entered into large scale trading activities since they had the necessary capital and power to employ the craftsmen. Localisation of crafts and their hereditary nature must have turned them into castes. Due to their wealth, the vaiśyas must have enjoyed some importance in the Orissan society during this period. There were evidences of rich vaiśyas of this period donating land to brāhmaṇas and temples.

Śūdras

According to the *Skanda Purāṇa* (*Utkala Khaṇḍa*) the śūdras of Orissa were described as being soft spoken and religious in nature. The śūdras, it further describes, served the brāhmaṇas. There is no direct reference to the śūdras in any of the inscriptions of this period. It is likely that the tribes, who entered into the brāhmaṇic fold as peasants and served to the higher castes, came to be known as śūdras. In the Bhauma records we find the terms[51] like *tantavāyas* (weavers), *saundhikas* (distiller), *gokūṭas* or *gauḍas* (cowherd) etc. which may be put into the śūdra castes. Many other functional castes like engravers, sculptors, masons and quarrymen etc. were existing during this period. On the basis of various representations of ornaments, weapons, pots etc., represented on the temples of our period, we can duduce the existence of *svarṇakāras* (goldsmith), *karmakāra* (blacksmith), *kumbhakāra* (potter), *pātakāra* (carpenter) etc. It is a fact that in order to prepare the copper-plates for the grants, the service of *kaṁsākāra* must have been required. We also get references of garland arranger (*pratihāra*), washerman, barber and gate-keeper from the records of this period.

The above-mentioned castes probably stayed as occupational groups initially, but in course of time were transformed into caste groups and were included in the śūdra caste.

Low Castes

Our information about the low castes is very inadequate. The *dohās*, written in proto-Oriya during this period, refer to *ḍomas*, and *cāṇḍālas* of Orissa. They were regarded as untouchables. Other untouchables include the *hāḍis*, the bamboomakers, the *pānas*, the *camāras* and the *dhobī* (washer-man). These castes lived outside the town or village.

Ibn Khurdādhba, a contemporary Arab geographer of the Bhaumakara period, mentioned that the Sandālia and *lehuḍ* were regarded as untouchables during this period.[52] Sandālia or *cāṇḍālas*, regarded as untouchables, also is known from the *Smṛtis* and *Dharmaśāstra*.[53] But the members of the *lehuḍ* community, who adopted music and dance as their professions, cannot be regarded as untouchables, as they performed dance in the houses of higher caste people. In all probability they were held in low esteem in the society of this period.

Aborigins

Though at present Orissa contains a very large and varied tribal population consisting of Bhuiyān, Gonḍs, Hos, Juāngs, Khonds, Orāons, Santālas, Savaras etc., only the *savaras* and Gonḍs figure in the epigraphic records of our period of study.

The *savaras* lived on hunting and went to distant places in search of quarry. In course of time by the tenth century AD, the brāhmanical culture had effected a process of social stratification and disintegration of the egalitarian internal structure of the aborigins.

Position of Women

According to the contemporary sources, it is known that the women of

Orissa during this period enjoyed an important position in society. General rules of the contemporary Hindu Society, did not usually permit women members to succeed to the throne. Only in case of a necessity, when the successor was a minor, the deceased queen assumed full control of the administration, only as regents. But the history of Bhaumakara dynasty gives a different picture. Here the queens were both *de jure* and *de facto* sovereigns. No less than six queens[54] are found to have adorned the Bhauma throne. Five of them were wives of kings and one, the daughter of a king and a reigning queen. Most probably adoption of sons was looked down upon by the members of this royal family. The peaceful rule of the queens proves that the people of Orissa had no reason to view the reign of female rulers with disfavour. The sovereign status of these ruling queens is evident from the imperial epithets *mahārājādhirāja*, *paramabhaṭṭāraka*, and *Parameśvara*, as born by them. These female rulers had the right to grant lands to the brāhmaṇas and religious establishments like the male rulers. The contribution of these female rulers to the cultural and political history of Orissa was very significant. The success of these queens, in the field of administration, shows that the ladies of the royal household were trained in the art of government and warfare.

It is difficult to find reason for the high status and position, enjoyed by the royal women in Orissa when it was not so in other parts of India. It is noteworthy that when the contemporary ruling dynasties in India did not have any women ruler, the Bhaumakara rule had six women rulers. Perhaps the aboriginal background of the ruling dynasty, which was improvised into kṣatriyas, is responsible for giving the higher status to the Bhauma queens. The other reason behind this phenomenon may be the influence of Buddhism on the royal families as well as the people of Orissa as Buddhism has sanctioned high position to the womenhood. Another point given by Biswarup Das[55] is that due to the growing popularity of the *śakti* cult in Orissa during this period that we find there were many women rulers.

It is significant to note that in many of the donative records, the donor, while mentioning his parents, whether he refers to his father or not, invariably mentions about his mother and records the gifts to gods for piety and welfare of his mother.

The examples of the Bhauma Queens seem to have influenced the attitude of the ruling dynasties and particularly queens in India in the later period. Thus we had Queen Diḍḍā ruling over Kashmir in the later half of tenth century AD.

We do not find any evidence of either *satī* or concubinage in this period. The Bhauma queens lived as widows after the death of their husbands. The system of *purdāh* (putting on veil by women) was also unknown in Orissa in this period as we do not find its reference, in any of the inscription or in temple sculptures. But we find the beginning of the institution of *devadāsīs* in this period. We get reference to it in the Ratnagiri copper-plate of Karanakesari of this period, which refers to the existence of *devadāsīs* in the Solānapura *mahāvihāra*.[56] We get atleast three generations of temple dancers from this inscription of the Somavaṁśī period, which followed the Bahumakara period.

Another significant reference we get from the Tālcher plate of Śivakara III is the existence of *Nunnery*, (Buddhist monastery meant for nuns only) in the Buddhist temple of Jayasrama *vihāra*.[57]

Marriage

The accounts of Ibn Khurdādhba and contemporary epigraphic records refer to intercaste marriages of the '*anuloma* form' in India during this period.[58] But we are not certain whether it was prevalent in Orissa. Poligamy was known and practised in the royal society in Orissa. From a later record of the Bhauma dynasty we come to know that King Śubhakaradeva I of this dynasty married two princesses viz. Gaurī Mahādevī and Vakula Mahādevī, which would prove the existence of Poligamy during this period.[59]

Food and Drink

People, particularly brāhmaṇas, perferred to take vegetarian food during this period. The cereals which were commonly used were rice, wheat and barley. Sweets, milk and fruits were also used. Non-vegetarian food was, by no means, unknown to the people. Drinking was also in vogue, as there were references of distillers of wine or *saundhikas* in the records of the Bhaumakaras.

Dress and Ornaments

The sculptures of this period give clear picture about the types of dresses used by both the males and females. The male dress consisted of a lower garment or *adhovasana* (*dhotī* in modern times) round the waist, whereas the female dress consisted of two garments, upper and lower, fastened by a girdle. The folds in the female garments are sometimes gathered, passed between legs and tucked in behind. Both male and female dresses have folds in the front and hang down to the knee or just below it. Sometimes the women were dressed in close fitting tunic. This was undoubtedly the dress of the dancing girls. Sometimes, women put only the lower garment thereby exposing the upper part of their bodies. The garments of the sculptures are usually ornamented with embrodery.

The sculptures of the Bhauma period have the representations of a variety of ornaments, used by both males and females. They were *kuṇḍala* (ear-ring), *ratnahāra* (necklace), *mekhalā* (girdle), *keyura* (armlet), *mañjirā* (foot ornament), *kankana* (bracelet) etc.

These ornaments were made of gold, silver, and set with pearls and diamonds. It seems that the use of costly ornaments was restricted to high and rich class people. The poor could hardly afford to wear such precious ornaments.

Different styles of hair dressing were prevalent in the society. Women like to keep curly hairs and fix flowers on the locks of their hair. For hair dressing mirrors and combs were used. Beautiful women coloured their feet with *yavaka*[60] (red dye called *alatā* in Oriya) and decorated their lips and cheeks with *patrānakura*[61] on special occasions. The males generally kept long hairs and used a tiara. Sandal paste and incense were used as perfumes by the rich people.

Education and Learning

The Bahumakara period was a glorious period from the point of view of education and learning. The Bhauma kings themselves were renowned scholars and always had the company of learned scholars.[62] Śubhakaradeva II granted a village for the upkeep of a college, established by some learned brāhmaṇas.[63] The Angul plate of Dharma Mahādevī has stated that Śāntikara II made scholars happy.[64] Śivakara IV is stated in his Tālcher plate to have 'sharp faculty of understanding the spirit of the text of the *śāstras*.[65] The Hindol plate of Śubhakaradeva III states that he acquired profound knowledge of the *Āgamāntas*.[66] Śivakara I sent to the Chinese King Te-tsang an autographed manuscript of the *Gaṇḍavyūha*, the last section of the *Avatamsaka*, dealing with the practice and vow of Bodhisattva Sāmantabhadra in the hands of Prajñā, who studied for sometimes at Ratnagiri.[67] Ratnagiri was an important centre of Buddhist *yoga* in the eight century AD. Orissa of that period was a great centre of Buddhist philosophy and *Yoga*. Many monasteries had *Yoga* in their course of study. In order to get training in *Yoga*, scholars from foreign countries came to Orissa during this period.

We have evidences to prove that there existed in this age several organised intitutions which were founded and maintained by the people, from the king down to common individuals.

Both brāhmaṇa and non-brāhamaṇa scholars and teachers used to move about holding debates and disputations, which might have improved the standard of philosophical and classical learning.

The inscriptions of this period say the proficiency of scholars in different secular subjects such as *Veda*s, History, Politics, Poetry, Logic, *Śāstra*s, Astronomy and *Smṛti*s etc. The most popular subject among the foreign scholars was *Yoga* philosophy. Numerous grants to the learned brāhmaṇas show that Vedic studies were encouraged during this period.

The popularity of Sanskrit language in Orissa during this period is clear from the use of Sanskrit in invariably all the inscriptions of the Bhaumakaras. The texts of the copper-plate inscriptions are composed partly in prose and partly in verse. The poetic skill of the authors is clearly marked from the ornate style of the verses. The mode of expressions has reached the excellence of *kāvya* writing, found in most of the famous works of Sanskrit literature, with reference to classical metres and figures of speech. The *śloka*s (lines of poetry) are full of long compounds. The use of simele, metaphor, paranomasia, alliteration etc. is found in every inscription in eulogising the kings or queens. In between *śloka*s prose lines are also found to occur which signifies that there was no hard and fast rule for the composition of prose and poetry.

A mild beginning of the Oriyā language was made during this period. Some of the Sanskrit names like *unmattasiṁha layanahāra*, *peṭṭapāla* have been represented in the inscriptions in their corrupt forms in *unmattsimha*, *lonabhāra padapāla*. These corruptions and such words as *thira* (*sthira*) *pruva* (*pūrva*), occurring in the inscriptions of this period suggest the influence of regional Prākṛt on Sanskrit and the gradual evolution of modern Oriyā language. We notice the use of some Oriyā words like *jota*, *gohiri* (fallow land), *khāta* (dump), *bāgha* (tiger), *kheta* (field), *vila* (field), *polla* (bridge) etc. in the Hindol plate of Śubhakara III and in the Tālcher plate of Śivakara III.

Thus from the point of view of education and learning the period of the Bhaumakaras was a glorious one.

CONTEMPORARY INDIAN SOCIETY

In order to compare the social conditions of Bengal and Orissa with that of contemporary India, we have to discuss in detail about various aspects of social behaviour in other parts of India during the period of our study.

Caste system

Caste was still not rigid as it is at present. Brāhmaṇas were distinguished by their *gotra*s and their *śākhā*. The *kula* (family background) of the kṣatriyas became important from this time and began to assume importance. *Gotra* and *pravara* lost importance with the kṣatriyas, who however, never lost respect for the *Veda*s and Vedic ordinary rituals.

The brāhmaṇas secured the highest position in the society. In the contemporary literature, this point has been highlighted. *Matsya Purāṇa* prescribes, for a brāhmaṇa, guilty of serious offences, banishment and branding with distinctive signs instead of death penalty. Going a step further Medhātithi, a writer of *Dharmaśāstras*, forbids not only corporal punishment, but even a money fine, to be inflicted upon a guilty brāhmaṇa.[68] The *Skanda Purāṇa* observes that he, who makes a gift to a brāhmaṇa, sacrifies the manes as well as gods. The *Smṛtis* of this period condemn brāhmaṇas of some particular types. *Varāha Purāṇa* gives long lists of brāhmaṇas who, because of their physical appearance or occupation or conduct, must not be invited to a funeral repast. The brāhmaṇas, again were degraded by residence in various lands. As *Matsya Purāṇa* says brāhmaṇas living in the *mleccha* countries of Triśaṅku, Barbara, Oḍra (Orissa), Andhra, Takka (Punjab), Draviḍa (Tamil Nāḍu) and Koṅkaṅa (Mahārāṣṭra) must not be invited to a funeral repast. The brāhmṇas were at liberty to take to professions of the lower castes, in addition to their own profession (the priestly). They were soldiers and government officers of high as well as low rank. They, no doubt, still kept the ban in the professions of learning. The inscriptions of this period describe the brāhmaṇa donees of lands as being devoted to the study of the *Vedas* and performed various religious duties. Al-masudi records,[69] "Brahmins are honoured as the most illustrious and noble caste". As royalty was confined to one family and the position of Vazir etc. were hereditary, the status of brāhmaṇs and kṣatriyas remained unchanged for a long period of time.

Thus brāhmaṇas and kṣatriyas were usually proficient in letters, and arms respectively. There was no objection to kṣatriyas studying the *Vedas* and the *śāstras*, as there were examples of kṣatriyas excelling in these branches of study. It appears from the *Parāśara Smṛti*, which may be assigned to this period, that during this period many brāhmaṇas and kṣatriyas took to agriculture because of forcible circumstances. The kṣatriyas, probably split up in consequence into two classes (1). the Rājpūts, i.e., the kings and rulers and (2). ordinary kṣatriyas or cultivators and land holders.

As the profession of agriculture, which mainly belonged to the śūdras, was allowed to brāhmaṇas and kṣatriyas, so the profession of arms, which mainly belonged to the kṣatriyas, was allowed to be shared by the brāhmaṇas and vaiśyas.

The high standard of life and conduct prescribed by the *Smṛti* laws was not always followed in actual practice. There were references to unworthy brāhmaṇas neglecting their ordinary duties and obligations.

The vaiśyas, had already lost touch with Vedic ritual, having turned Buddhists in far greater number than the higher two castes. Hence they have not preserved the memory of their *gotras*.

Besides brāhmaṇas, kṣtriyas and vaiśyas, another important caste which was mentioned very often in the literature of this period, was the kāyastha caste as writer of inscriptions. These kāyasthas, too, were apparently one caste throughout India, and had not yet split up into sub-divisions, as at present. This caste was included in the *Vedavyāsa-smṛti*'s list of śūdra castes.[70]

According to Medhātithi,[71] sons of twice-born classes, born out of women of lower *varṇa*s, other than śūdras, are entitled to the ceremony of initiation and enjoy all the privileges of a twice-born man. The caste of *karana*, derived from the union of vaiśya males with śūdra women is included among śūdra castes in the *Bṛhad-dharma Purāṇa*.[72]

According to a text of Parāśara,[73] eating a śūdra's food, association with a śūdra, sitting on the same seat with a śūdra, and taking lessons from a śūdra by a person of higher caste are acts of serious offence. According to an un-named *Smṛti*, a twice-born man, on touching a śūdra must purify himself by ceremonial sipping of water.[74] *Laghu-vyāsa* forbids the *Veda* to be taught in the vicinity of śūdras.[75] Medhātithi, says that a śūdra does nothing wrong if, being a possessor of wealth, he lives without dependence upon a brāhmaṇa. This shows that he recognises the śūdra's absolute right to personal freedom. Medhātithi observes that śūdra incurs sin only if he commits acts that are prohibited to him (i.e, the śūdra is not entitled to initiation and similar sacraments).[76]

Agni Purāṇa declares that *cāṇḍāla*s shall be employed for the execution of criminals and they must live outside the village and must not touch others or not to throw their shadows upon others.

Brahmāṇḍa Purāṇa says that one should bathe with his clothes on after touching heretical sects like Śaivas, Pāśupatas, Lokāyatikas and others. Another text *Śattrimanmālā* mentions that one should do the same if he touches *Bauddhas* (Buddhists), Pāśupatas, Laukāyatikas.[77]

The lower castes or *antyajātis* were seven in number according to Vaijayanti. They are washermen, leather workers, fishermen, *venas*, *burulas*, *medas* and *bhillas*.[78] Among these *venas*, *burulas*, *medas* and *bhillas* were aboriginal tribes, while the rest were occupational groups of the lowest order.

Marriages

Nāradīya Purāṇa declares that marriages of twice-born men with girls of other *varṇas* are forbidden. According to Medhātithi, in case of marriages in the natural order (*anuloma*), the son takes the caste of the mother, and in case of marriages in the reverse (*pratiloma*) order, he takes the caste of the father. Marriage appears to have been restricted generally to the caste itself. But Ibn Khurdādhba remarks, one exception viz. that the brāhmaṇa could marry a daughter of a kṣatriya. Probably the kṣatriya also claimed a similar privilege and married vaiśya wives. Formerly, by the *Manu Smṛti*, the brāhmaṇa could marry kṣatriya, vaiśya and śūdra wives. But in this period the marriage of a śūdra women by a brāhmaṇa or generally by the higher caste was prohibited.

Marriage by mutual love (*Gāndharva Vivāha*) is ensured by Medhātithi.[79] He says girls should be given away in marriage when they are eight or six years old, called *nagnikā* and one should marry a girl very much younger than himself. A girl should stay in her father's house for three years after attaining puberty and then if she is not given marriage by her guardian, she may choose her husband without fear of sin.

As regards re-marriage of women, *Agni Purāṇa*[80] says that a woman is permitted to take a second husband in the event of five calamities viz. when the husband is lost, or is dead, or has adopted the life of a recluse, or is impotent, or has become an outcaste.

It appears that marriages were often arranged by parents or other guardians of the parties. Sometimes girls, with the approval of their parents, choose their husbands at a '*swayaṁvara* ceremony'.

The polygamous habit of Indian kings is proved by contemporary inscriptions. Husband and wife were generally separated by death, as divorce was generally not allowed.

Position of Women

The literature of this period emphasise the duty of absolute obedience and devotion of wives to their husbands. In case of separation of husband and wife, due to misunderstanding, wife had the right to maintenance from her husband.

The king's wives and queens in north India were not seen in open court. In other castes *purdāh* was not strict.

The widow is entitled to succeed to the whole property of her sonless deceased husband, provided she is chaste.

The political influence of royal ladies can be traced during this period especially in the records of the Deccan and south India.

The dread rite of *satī* at this time was enjoined by some authorities but condemned by others. According to the Arab writer Sulaiman,[81] wives of kings sometimes burnt themselves on the funeral pyres of their husbands, but it was for them to excercise their option in the matter. It seems from descriptions of the prevailing literature that this custom was not confined to the royal family only, as becoming *satī* was recognised as one of the virtues of a wife. The custom of royal servants of kings, sacrificing their lives for their masters and burning themselves when they died, is noticed by Arab travellers during this period.

From the description of Medhātithi and the inscriptions of this period, it becomes clear that the custom of dedicating maidens for service in temples were continued in this period.[82] The number of these girls in temples often reached high proportions.

The class of prostitutes, known from early times, existed as a distinct social unit in the present age. *Matsya Purāṇa* lays down a list of their duties and rights as well as the special clauses of law applicable to them.[83]

Medhātithi observes that women should have no freedom of action regarding the great objects of human existence (viz. virtue, wealth and pleasure) but should obtain permission of their husbands or other male relations before spending money on such acts. Women should be restrained from singing and similar acts.

Ornaments and Dress

Ladies of high families delighted in the display of ornaments by habit. Rājśekhara describes that the queen's limbs were anointed with saffron and her eyes with collyrium, her lovely locks well arranged, her hair was decorated with flowers, while her person was adorned with ear-ring, rows of bracelets, ruby encrusted girdle, and emerald anklets. The queen at night time appears in a robe of Chinese silk with a pearl necklace around her neck, camphor powder on her bosom, and sandal paste thickly applied to her limbs. According to Sulaiman, an Arabian traveller, Indians, both male and female, adorned themselves with golden bracelets.[84] But using of costly ornaments was only restricted to the upper class women. The common people used ornaments made of cheap materials.

Food and Drink

Al Masudi writes, "The Hindus abstain from drinking wine and censure those who consume it". *Viṣṇudharmottara* mentions ten kinds of wines which are forbidden to brāhmaṇas, but permitted to kṣatriyas and vaiśyas.[85] Medhātithi says that while brāhamaṇa women did not drink wine at festivals, kṣatriya and other women, to whom drinking was not forbidden, indulged in excessive drinking when they gathered together on festive occasions. Though the kṣatriyas were not bound by religious precept to abstain from wine, but it was a fact that most of them abstained. The vaiśyas were total abstainers, though there must have some exception.

The brāhmaṇas were generally abstainers from flesh, though not quite completely. But it seems that in sacrifices which were becoming rare and in *śrāddhas* (annual ceremonies remembering dead persons) which were still performed, flesh was necessarily served not only among kṣatriyas but among brāhmaṇas and vaiśyas also. The brāhmaṇas were neither allowed to drink the milk of any animal but cow and she-buffalo, nor to eat onions and other bad vegetables.

There was general prohibition against beef and the flesh of larger animals like tigers. The *cāṇḍalas* or outcastes alone did not observe this prohibition. Medhātithi lays down at great length the occasions on which the eating of meat is lawful. It appears from his description that the peacock, the horse, the white ass, the female sparrow, the wild cock and the wild pig counted distinctly as lawful food, while certain kinds of web-footed and fish eating birds were classed optionally as such.

Brahma Purāṇa declares a number of herbs and vegetables as well as cereals to be forbidden food.

The different higher castes had no objection to take food at one another's house. The only condition is one must know the family, with whom one eats, to be a *dvija* (upper cates) family. The *Smṛti* allows the taking of food by *dvijas* with the following śūdras viz. barbers, friends of the family, servants and cowherds.

Games and Amusements

It was the fashion for high born girls to play with balls (*kanduka*). In the spring season and on the occasion of the swing festival, they used to enjoy the swing from trees in a garden. Dancing for recreation by ladies and dramatic representations in honour of deities are referred to in the inscriptions of the period. In Rājaśekhara's account of a poet's daily life we read that he used to arrange a poetical assembly (*kāvyagoṣṭhī*) everyday after his midday meal.[87]

Standard of Living

The high standard of living, which appears to have prevailed at least among the upper classes in the preceding period, was well maintained during this period.

The standard of living among the upper classes especially royal classes was fairly high. We have references of kings having very magnificent places with all the luxurious items in them. They change their residences according to seasons. The royal processions, as described by foreign authors, were marked by equal gorgeousness.

Beliefs and Superstitions, Manners and Customs

The old belief in Omens and in astrology continued to have its hold on the people. Ban against sea voyage was repeated during this period. But this restriction was hardly followed in the time of necessity and conquests. We have evidence that king Rājendra Cola I sent a naval expedition on AD 1025 for the conquest of the Sailendra empire of Sumātrā and the Malāya Peninsula.

There was custom of employment of large number of female attendants in the king's service.

A custom prevailing in south India during this period was that of self-immolation of selected nobles on the funeral pyres of their kings.

Thus the social conditions of India, outside the periphery of Bengal and Orissa were more or less similar to that of Bengal and Orissa. The only exception was the status of women. In Bengal and Orissa, the position of women was very higher as compared to that of other parts of India.

Notes

1. Rislay (i) *The people of India*, (ii) *The Tribes and Castes of Bengal*, I-XV ff.
2. Edited in *Bibliotheca Indica* series.
3. The lists of the *Varṇasaṅkara* has been taken from the *History of Bengal*, Vol. I, by R.C. Majumdar, pp. 568-70.
4. R.C. Majumdar (ed.), *The History of Bengal*, pp. 574-75.
5. Kane, *History of Dharmaśāstra*, Vol. II, Ch. II, pp. 52 ff. 447 ff.
6. M. Chakravarti, *JASB*, 1915 pp. 327-36.
7. *IHQ*, VI, pp. 55-56.
8. R.C. Majumdar (ed.), *History of Bengal*, p. 585.
9. *Ibid.*, pp. 585-86.
10. S.C. Das (ed.), Introd. p. III.
11. R.C. Majumdar (ed.), *History of Bengal*, p. 588.
12. *Ibid.*, p. 589.

13. *Ibid.*, pp. 590-91.
14. Girish Chandra Vidyaratha (ed.), *Prāyaścitta-Prakaraṇa*, p. 118.
15. Beal, Records II, pp. 194-204.
16. *Mitakshara*, Nirnayasāgara edition, p. 257.
17. Manomohan Chakravarti (ed.), *JASB*, 1905, pp. 53-71.
18. *Ibid.*
19. *Bṛhad-dharma Purāṇa*, II Vol. 8, p. 3-10.
20. Girishchandra Vidyaratha (ed.), *Prāyaścitta Prakaraṇa* of Bhaṭṭa Bhavadeva, p. 67.
21. *Ibid.*, p. 66.
22. *Ibid.*
23. *Ibid.*, p. 65.
24. *Ibid.*
25. *Pavanadūta*, vv. 40, 42, 43, 44.
26. *BGD*, 44, 49.
27. *Pavanadūta*, vv, 33, 38.
28. R.C. Majumdar (ed), *History of Bengal*, p. 610
29. R.C. Majumdar, Basak and N.G. Banerji (ed.), *Rāmacarita*, Vol. III, vv, 5-28.
30. *Pavanadūta* vv. 36 ff.
31. R.C. Majumdar (ed.), *History of Bengal*, p. 619-20.
32. *GL*, p. 71.
33. R.C. Majumdar (ed.), *History of Bengal,* (Vol. I) p. 305.
34. *Ibid.*, p. 311.
35. *Ibid.*, p. 320.
36. *Ibid.*, p. 322.
37. *Ibid.*, p. 323.
38. Colebrooke (tr.) in English, Reprint, Calcutta, 1910.
39. Austosh Mookherjee (ed.) in *Memoris of ASB*, II, No. 5, Calcutta, 1910-14.
40. *Bibliographica Indica* (ed.) Calcutta, 1905.
41. *EI*, Vol. XV, p. 3.
42. *EI*, Vol. XV, p. 213.
43. *Matsya Puraṇa* written in the fourth to fifth century AD.
44. They are Sārasvata, Kānyakubja, Utkala (old name of Orissa), Maithila and Gauḍa.

45. *Skanda Purāṇa* (*Utkala Khaṇḍa*), Vol. VI, pp. 10-11.
46. S. Beal, *Buddhist Records of Western World*, Vol. II, p. 209.
47. *JBORS*, Vol. V, p. 569.
48. *JBORS*, Vol. XIV, Part-II, p. 297.
49. R.S. Sharma, *Social Changes in Early Medieval India*, pp. 14-15.
50. S. Jaiswal, Charges in the status and concept of Sudra Varna in Early Medieval Ages, In *PIHC*, Vol. XLI, p. 112.
51. *JBORS*, Vol. II, pp. 426-27.
52. A.S. Altekar, *Rāṣṭrakūṭas and their times*, 1967, p. 320.
53. P.V. Kane, *History of the Dharma-Śāstra*, II, i, p. 48.
54. The queens were Tribhuvana Mahādevī I, Pṛthvī Mahādevī *alias* Tribhuvana Mahādevī-II, Gaurī Mahādevī, Daṇḍi Mahādevī, Vakula Mahādevī, and Dharma Mahādevī.
55. B. Das, *The Bhaumakaras and Their Time*, p. 77.
56. D.C. Sircar, *Studies in society and Administration in Ancient and Medieval India*, Vol. I, p. 243.
57. B. Mishra, *Orissa under the Bhauma Kings*, p. 42.
58. Elliots and Dowson, *History of India as told by its own historians* I, London, 1870.
59. *EI*, XXVIII, Part-IV, p. 257.
60. *IHQ*, Vol. XXI, pp. 221 ff.
61. B. Mishra, *Orissa Under the Bhauma Kings*, p. 47.
62. *JBORS*, Vol. II, pp. 419 ff.
63. *EI*, Vol. XXVII, p. 214.
64. *JAS*, Vol. XVII, No. 3, pp. 18 ff.
65. B. Mishra, *Orissa Under the Bhauma Kings*, p. 34 ff.
66. *Ibid.*, p. 18.
67. Bhupindranath Dutta, *Mystic Tales of Lama Taranath*, pp. 48-49.
68. *Age of Imperial Kanauj*, ed. by R.C. Majumdar, p. 369.
69. *History of Medieval Hindu India Vol. II*, C.V. Vaidya, p. 181.
70. *Age of Imperial Kanauj*, p. 371.
71. On Manu, X 41.
72. *Age of Imperial Kanauj*, p. 371.

73. *Saṁskāra Prakāśa*, p. 513.
74. *Age of Imperial Kanauj*, p. 370.
75. *Saṁskāra Prakāśa*, p. 525.
76. On Manu, X, 126.
77. *Age of Imperial Kanauj*, p. 372.
78. *The Struggle for Empire*, p. 476.
79. On Manu, VIII, p. 366.
80. CLIV-5.
81. *HIED*, I, ii.
82. *Age of Imperial Kanauj*, p. 374.
83. *Ibid.*
84. *Ibid.*, p. 384.
85. *Ibid.*, p. 385.
86. *EI*,V.23, IAXII-13.
87. *Age of Imperial Kanauj*, p. 385.

5

Economic Conditions in Bengal and Orissa

BENGAL DURING PĀLA PERIOD

IT is very difficult to reconstruct the economic history of ancient and early medieval Bengal, because of scanty availability of source materials. In order to study the economic history of a particular region, we depend mostly on the court rolls, the guild rolls, the pipe rolls and the craft ordnances and statutes of the rulers of that region. But unfortunately no such thing is available in Bengal.

A large number of inscriptions belonging to different dynasties reveal that during the fifth and sixth centuries AD there existed in Bengal a class of officers called *pustapāla*s or record keepers who were attached both to the villages and district headquarters, and whose obvious business was to maintain records of lands with their boundaries, demarcations and titles. But it is a misfortune that not a fragment of these valuable records, written perhaps on palm leaves, has come down to us. In the absence of these records, all that we can do is to glean a few isolated facts concerning the economic condition of the people from such fragmentary sources of information as archaeology, occasional notices contained in literature, and the accounts of foreign travellers and historians.

Rural Settlements

The most significant fact with the economic history of Bengal was the preponderance of rural settlements. The people lived in the villages and established themselves there. They organised their lands (the fields, meadow and woodlands) to serve their essential needs. The contemporary inscriptions mentioned the names of a large number of villages. The villages varried considerably in size, but they seem to have been all alike in their close dependence in the utilization of the soil on which they stood. All the villages appeared to have been of one uniform pattern. They were usually of the nucleated, not of the single form type. This means the rural population lived in compact groups and not in widely scattered habitations. The nucleated village is best suited to an agrarian system in which cultivation prominently figures.

The inscriptions of this period reveal that the villages usually consisted of certain well defined parts, viz. village settlement or habitat (*vastu*), arable land (*kṣetra*) and natural meadow land (*go-cara*), the pasture of live stock. The term *tṛṇa-pūti-go-cara-paryantaḥ*, mentioned frequently in most of the Pāla records, suggests that the pasture ground produced various kinds of grass and was usually located in a corner of the village. Apart from this, most of the villages contained pits and canals (*gārta* or *nālā*) which might have served the purpose of drainage; barren tracts (*ūsara*); tanks; reservoirs and temples; besides cattle tracts (*go-patha*) and ordinary roads and paths. A few villages are also stated to have been in possession of woodlands or jungles,[1] where the common folk probably went to gather their fire wood and litter. It is thus clear that the various types of land in the villages were not only distinguished and classified from the point of view of their usefulness to man, but were organised for exploration according to certain systems and customary practices so as to best satisfy human needs.

Urban Settlements

It is a fact that Bengal was primarily a land of villages, but that does not mean that there were no towns or urban settlements in the period of our study. Many factors contributed to the rise of urban centres. The trade centres, the capital cities and the religious centres in course of time became cities. An analysis of the sites and positions occupied by the towns in early medieval Bengal shows that they were of such a geographical character that they could be utilised as centres of routes by lands or by water.

It is strange to note that the early Pāla inscriptions did not mention about the location of the metropolies of that time. We have ony reference to a few camps of victory mostly in the neighbouring provinces of Bihar.[2] In the time of Dharmapāla, who was referred to as *vaṅgapati* in a Pratihāra record, the ancestral capital may have been in Eastern Bengal. But from the time of Devapāla, who is styled as *gauḍeśvara* (King of Gauḍa) in the Bādāl Pillar inscription, Gauḍa seems to have been the metropolitan *viṣaya* (district). *Anargha-rāghava* a literary work of Murāri, who probably flourished in the latter part of the eighth century AD, refers to Campā as the capital of Gauḍa. The connection of Campā with a Pāla King of Gauḍa has been inferred from the Jaynagar Image Inscription. Campā in Gauḍa may have been identified with the Campā-nagarī in the Sarkar (sub-division) of Madāran mentioned in the *Āin-i-Akbarī* of Abul Fazl. It may however also refer to the famous city of that name that stood near modern Bhāgalpur.

Epigraphic records of the time of Gopāla II, Mahipāla I and Vigrahapāla III refer to royal encampments of Vaṭāpar, Vāṭika, Valāsapura, and Haradhāma.[3] The last two camps were situated on the Gaṅgās, as the royal donors bathed in the sacred stream before issuing grants, found mention in the records from these places.

Rāmapāla, the youngest son of Vigrahapāla III, gave his name to the city Rāmāvatī, mentioned in the Manahali records of Madanapāla and *Rāmacarita* of Sandhyākara.

Among the less known dynasties that ruled contemporaneously with the Pālas in the tenth and eleventh centuries AD, the Kāmbojas of Daṇḍabhukti had their capital at Priyangu, which is not satisfactorily identified. The Candras and Varman families issued grants from the victory camps at Vikramapura and were associated with the cities of Rohitagiri, Paṭṭikerā, Mehārakula and Siṁhapurā.

The religious-cum-academic centres of this period, which became very famous cities in course of time were Nālandā, Odantapuri, Vikramaśilā, Tāmralipti and many other places.

The differences between rural and urban centres have been the same all over medieval India. Both literary and epigraphic evidences make it clear that the rural population was mainly dependent on the soil and its produce, but urban centres, although not wholly unattached to the agricultural activity, tended to serve a wide variety of functions like commercial, industrial, political, judicial and military. The most distinguished characteristic of the urban centres was their comparative richness and luxury.

Land Tenures and Tax System

In India land is the main support of life throughout the ages. So medieval Bengal was no exception to it. Land was the main source of wealth. We have no clear-cut knowledge about the land tenure in Bengal under the Pālas. Most of the early copper-plate grants refer to the sale or gift of waste land for pious purposes. Although the state sold away plots of land out of the unappropriated waste, it still reserved to itself certain rights over the property. The purchaser or the donee was allowed only the (usufructuary) right to use the land and enjoy over the profit and not the land. The holdings were governed by a law, described in the contemporary documents as *nivi-dharma*.[4] Whether all holdings in the country were regulated by the law of the *nivi-dharma* is not known to us. However, the probability is that it applied only the estates created for pious purposes.[5] It is also not definitely known whether land alienated by sale or gift under this form of tenure were rent-free or "became liable to a progressive enhancement of the revenue, till the normal rate was reached" as Dr. Ghosal suggests.[6] There are sufficient reasons to believe that immunity from taxation was one of the privileges enjoyed by the assignee in such cases.

Inscriptions belonging to the Pālas and other contemporary dynasties of Bengal give a different picture as regards to the pious endowments. The religious endowments with rare exceptions, were made by kings and rich individuals in favour of temples and religious foundations, of individuals like priests and learned brāhmaṇas and sometimes of institutions and persons combined. The conditions and immunities attaching to these grants are found enumerated in the copper-plate charters which resistered them. For example, the Khālimpur plate of Dharmapāla records the grant of four villages with the immunity from penalties for the ten offences (*sa-daśāpacārāh*), with the immunity from all the burdens (*parihṛta-sarva-pīḍāh*), with the immunity from all the taxes (*akiñcit-pragrāhyāh*), according to the maxim of the uncultivable land (*bhūmicchidra-nyāyena*) and to last as long as the sun, moon and earth shall endure.[7] In addition to all these concessions, the donee was to receive all those taxes in kind or in cash which the cultivators in the alienated villages had hither to paid to the sovereign. The right to forced labour (*pīḍā*), that of punishing thieves (*sa-caura-dhāraṇa*), of dealing with the commission of ten offences (*sa-daśāpacārāh*) are transferred to the grantee.[8]

Thus it is obvious that these were grants in perpetuity, rent-free and accompanied with the assignment of all revenues accruing to the crown. But what is not clear, however is whether they made over to the donee merely the state share of the produce and other state rights in the land alienated or conveyed to him the proprietorship of the land as well, that is, an out and out gift of soil and revenue both.[9]

It is to be noted that these beneficial tenures, called *śāsanas* and *agrahāras* in contemporary records, never covered more than a fraction of the agricultural land. They did not touch the mass of the cultivators in the state.

We have no knowledge about the pattern of rights of the cultivators on the soil, they tilled. From the copper-plate charters only this much can be inferred that some of the cultivators were non-proprietary or exproprietary tenant.[10] It is certain that all or most of the cultivators had to pay various kinds of taxes and local cesses. Besides the payment of taxes and cesses the holding of land seems to have entailed various other obligations. These included certain services which the cultivators had occasionally to render to an army passing to the cultivators area such as provision of quarters, supply of provisions or labour and provision of food on the occasion of a king of high official visiting the locality and the prerequisite paid on the occasion of the birth of a prince, marriage of a princess etc. (milk money). These were not regular taxes, but customary dues paid on specific occasions.

The landgrants indicate that the possession of land carried with it certain inherent privileges which included the right to everything under the ground and above it such as mines, salt, wood, bush and trees including fruits. Whenever any plot of land is given away accurate details are furnished not merely with regards to boundaries but also matters relating to its economic value as well. Every copper-plate grant was to be stamped with the royal seal before handing over to the donee.

The officer *śāṣthādhikṛta* was incharge of levying tax on the produce of the land. The cultivators and others paid different types of taxes like *bhāga*, *bhoga*, *kara*, *hiraṇya* etc. (*bhāga-bhoga-kara-hiraṇya ādi sarva pratyay o pāpanāyaḥ*).[11] There were different classes of officers for collecting revenues from different sources. The agricultural taxes were collected through the heads of territorial units such as *upārika*, *viṣayapati*, *daśagrāmika* and *grāmapati*. The tax levied on the villages for protection against thieves and robbers was collected by *cauroddhāraṇika*, customs and tolls were collected by *saulkika*, fine for criminal offences was collected by *daśāparādhika* and the ferry-duties were collected by *tārika*.

Agriculture

In most of the cases the land donated to various religious institutions and learned persons were *aprada* (unsettled), *aprahata* (uncultivated) and *khila* (fallow). Sometimes the waterlogged waste lands paying no tax, reported the copper-plates, were donated.[12] Even there were examples of forest regions being donated to religious institutions.[13] These instances of land donations show that many areas of uncultivated, waste land came under cultivation. Thus there was constant extension of cultivation, and rural settlement. The pressure of a growing population, the growing desire of priests for material prosperity and the religious zeal of the kings, all served in various ways for the occupation of the waste land and the extension of agriculture.

The copper-plate inscriptions of the period from eighth to twelfth century AD, mention the cultivators (*kṣetrakarāḥ* or *karṣakāḥ*) as an improtant class apart from the officials and brāhmaṇas. Thus it conveyed an idea of the important role they played in the economic life of the community.

The food crops grown in Bengal included paddy, sugarcane, mastard, betelnut, palm (*guvaka*), coconut (*nārikela*) and cotton. The fruits like mango (*āmra*), bread fruit (*paṇasa*), plantain (*kelā*), date (*kharjūra*), figs (*parkaṭi*), etc. were also widely cultivated.[14]

Measures of Land

From the landgrants of the Gupta period we get the mention of two technical terms viz. *kulyavāpa* and *droṇavāpa* in connection with land measurement, but in the absence of adequate data, their equivalents in modern measures cannot be determined. The actual work of measurement was done by means of *nalas* (reeds). According to F.E. Pargiter, *kulyavāpa* is just a little larger than an acre of land.[15] As time passed, the word *kulyavāpa* fell out of use and other technical terms of land measure gradually came into vogue. Of these the one denoting the largest unit of measure was the term *pātaka* or *bhū-pātaka*, which is frequently mentioned in the inscriptions found between eighth to twelfth century AD.

In the *Gunaighar Grant of Vainyagupta* (AD 507), we get the reference to the term *pātaka* for the first time. This plate mentions that a *pātaka* is equivalent to forty *droṇas* or *droṇavāpas* in area. From this we can ascertain that the *pātaka* was five times as big as the *kulyavāpa*.[16] Besides *pātaka* and *droṇa*, other terms used in the post-Gupta period records of Bengal, indicating the measurement of land, are *ādhaka* and *ādhavāpa*, *unmāna* or *udāna*, *kāka* or *kākinika*. Unfortunately the actual meaning of these terms is not yet known to us.

The system of measurement of landgrants during the Pāla period was very accurate and well developed. This could have been possible under an administration that paid due attention to surveys of land for purposes of taxation and also to the necessity of preserving all relevant documents bearing on the history of any assignment that might be contemplated. An unique feature of this system was followed in a particular area where the grant might have been situated. It is very unfortunate that no inscription of this period had mentioned about the measurement of the land.

Crafts and Industries

Although agriculture played an important role in the economy of Bengal, a number of crafts and industries also played important part in the life of the people. There were so many industries in Bengal during this period which included textile, sugar, metal work, stone work, wood work and pottery.

The textile and sugar industries made considerable headway from a very early period. The manufacture of salt by means of evaporation was very well-known in Bengal. The *Irdā* plate of the tenth century AD records the grant of a village in the Daṇḍabhukti-maṇḍala of the Vardhamāna-bhukti, along with its saltpits (*lavaṇakarah*).[17] Similarly the Rāmapāla plate of Śrīcandra[18] of the eleventh century AD and the Belāva plate of Bhojavarman[19] of the twelfth century AD mentions the grant of villages, located in the Puṇḍrabukti along with salt. Surprisingly no Pāla land-grant mentioned about salt manufacture in Bengal. From this we can infer that although the manufacture of salt was known and practised in certain places, it had not developed into any considerable industry. The damp climate and the discharged fresh water of the Gaṅgās into the sea might have hampered the growth of any large scale salt manufacture.

Pottery was a very prospering industry at that time. It was practised on an extensive scale. A large number of specimens of the pottery, used by the monks of Pahārpur dating back to eighth and ninth centuries AD, have been recovered in recent years. These include large storage jars, spotted vases or *loṭās*, cooking utensils, dishes, saucers, inkpots and lamps of various designs. The discovery of immense variety of terracotta plaques at Mahāsthān (Bogra), Sābhār (Dacca), Pahārpur and some other places prove beyond doubt the richnèss of this industry in Bengal during the period of our study. Even we get reference to potters[20] (*kumbhakāra*), and potter's ditch (*kumbhakāra-gārta*)[21] in some of the contemporary inscriptions. Pottery as an industry was conducted from rural settlements.

Along with pottery metal works of various kinds were practised in Bengal. As Bengal was predominantly agricultural based, the importance of the blacksmith in preparing various agricultural implements has been great. Contemporary evidences prove that apart from agricultural implements, the black smiths manufactured other articles of general use like water vessels of iron,[22] and weapons of war such as arrow-heads, spear-heads and swords.[23] Besides working in iron, the metal workers practised the art of bronze-casting with considerable skill. This is proved by the discovery of a large number of bronze or acto-alloy images in different parts of Bengal.

Jewellery provided an important occupation to a considerable number of people, for it was the fashion of the rich to use gold and silver dishes and ornaments, studded with pearls and precious stones.

Another important craft was the stone and wood carving. The numerous stone images discovered in Bengal and the beautifully engraved inscriptions on stone slabs bear the testimony both to the volume and skill of the stone carvers profession. It has been suggested that the black chlorite stone out of which most of these images were carved, was probably obtained from the Rājmahal hills and carried in boats to the different sculptor's art in the province.[24] Along with stone carving, wood carving and carpentary also appear to have been practised on an extensive scale. But owing to the perishable nature of wood, only a few architectural specimens of wood carving of pre-Muhammadan period have come down to us. It appears that the wood workers built houses, temples and also manufactured household furniture, boats, ships and wheeled carriages.[25]

Another important industry which flourished during this time was ivory carving. Other minor arts, crafts, professions and industries may be mentioned those of scribes, florists, conch-shell worker, braziers, goldsmiths, painters, masons, oilmen, fishermen, washermen, barbers, butchers, distillers of wine etc., who formed so many distinct castes.[26]

We hardly know anything definite about the nature and organisation of industrial labour. From certain statements in the inscriptions here and there, we can infer that the workers in various trades, crafts and industries were organised into some kind of corporate groups. Four copper-plate inscriptions found at Damodarpur[27] in Bengal of the fifth and sixth centuries AD mention about the position occupied by the *nagara-śreṣṭhi* (guild president), *prathama sārthavāha* (chief merchant) and *prathama-kulika* (the chief artisan) in the local administration. Similarly the Deopārā inscriptions of Vijayasena refers to Ranaka Sulapāni, who engraved the stone, as 'Varendra-*śilpigoṣṭhi-cūḍāmaṇi*' (crest jewel of the guild of Varendra artists), which suggests that guild was very much prevalent during that time.[28] Though the inscriptions of the Pālas were silent about the guilds, that does not mean that these were not existing at that time as it was there before as well as after the Pāla period.

Trade

There was prosperity in the trade and commerce of Bengal during this period. This qualitative and quantitative development of Bengal's industries and the vast sea coast and river systems of the province, seem to be the main reasons of the growth of trade and commerce.

Internal Trade

Neither of the inscriptions of this period nor the foreign accounts deal much about the inland trade for which we have very little knowledge about the internal trade of this period in Bengal. The mention of *hāṭṭa-pati*, *saulkika* and *tārika* (officers-in-charge of markets, customs, tolls and ferries) in the landgrants indirectly testifies the brisk nature of internal trade. This also shows that the state derived a considerable revenue from this.

The principal centres of inland trade were towns though a certain amount of business was done in the villages also. The Khālimpur plate of Dharmapāla records the grant of four villages along with their *haṭṭika*, which according to Kielhorn,[29] means 'market dues'.

The main routes of internal trade were probably the water ways, in proximity to which stood the principal towns. Apart from the rivers, a certain amount of trade passed through the land routes also. The early Bengali *caryāpadas* frequently refer to boats, including sea going vessels. The camel was used as means of conveyance in Bengal.

Foreign Trade

There was brisk foreign trade in Bengal, during this period. The port cities of Tāmralipti and Saptagrāma were main centres of foreign trade. From the Tāmralipti port radiated three main overseas routes for trading activities. The first one led in a south-easternly direction past the coast of Ārākan to Burma and beyond. The second line was with the Mālāya peninsula and the far East. A third line of trade led in a south-westernly direction past the coasts of Kaliṅga and Coromaṇḍala to south India and Ceylon.

Besides the sea-routes, there seem to have been a number of land routes through, which Bengal's foreign trade was carried. One of these routes was the route which connected, Puṇḍravardhana with Kāmarūpa along which Hiuen-Tsang journeyed in the seventh century AD.[30] Kāmarūpa was famous for her textiles, sandal and agaru and it seems that these items were taken to the main centres of business in northern India along this high way of traffic. This route seems to have extended beyond Kāmarūpa to south China throgh the hills of Manipur and upper Burma. A rock inscription of the chief named Udayamāna of the eighth century AD, reveals that merchants from Ayodhyā used to frequent the port of Tāmralipti for purposes of trade.[31]

Another land route led through the passes of the Himālayas, past Sikkim to Tibet and China. This route became the great highway of Buddhist pilgrim travel between Magadha and Tibet. Towards the end of twelfth century AD horses in large numbers appear to have been imported into Bengal along this track. Another overland route ran southwards, along the Kaliṅga Coast (modern Orissa) to the south Indian Peninsula.[32]

Medium of Exchange

It is not very much known when the metallic coin was introduced in Bengal. But it is almost certain that the metallic coins were known and used several centuries before the commencement of the Christian era.

When the Pālas established their dominance over Bengal and Bihar firmly, they made an attempt to reintroduce minted currency in their area. But this currency was discontinued after some time because of political instability in Bengal. This is known by the discovery of a few copper and silver coins, belonging to the Pāla period. Three copper coins of a unique type of bull on the obverse and three fish on the reverse have been found at Pahārpur, assigned to the early Pāla period. From the legend *śrī vigra* on the obverse side of the coins found in Bengal and Bihar, these are attributed to King Vigrahapāla, a Pāla monarch. The coins are popularly known as Vigrahapāla *dhamma*, the term *dhamma* as a designation of coins, occurring in the Bodh Gayā inscription of Dharmapāla.

From the extreme scarcity and generally debased character of these coins, it seems that the attempt of the Pāla rulers to introduce a currency of their own was a faint hearted one and was soon abandoned. It is surprising to see such meagre amount of currency under the Pālas considering that they had a great empire and a long rule of prosperity and stability.

The existence of a type of silver coin called *dramma*, is proved by a reference contained in the Mahābodhi inscription of the 26th regnal year of Dharmapāla. In this inscription it was mentioned that the cost of the excavation of a tank would be three thousand *drammas*.[33] It may be possible that Vigrahapāla's *dhamma* and Dharmapāla's *dramma* were the different names of the same silver coin.

ORISSA DURING THE BHAUMAKARA PERIOD

The civilization of a state depends a great deal on the economic prosperity achieved by it. During the period of our study, Orissa was economically in a sound position.

We notice a tendency for the growth of feudalism in Orissa during the Bhaumakara period. The ruling family granted lands to feaudal vassals, officials, temples and above all to brāhmaṇas which led to the fragmentation of land in Orissa. The grants consisted of religious as well as secular assignees.

The secular grantees consisted of vassals and officials. But the brāhmaṇa donees far out numbered the secular assignees. The Bhauma ruler Śivakara[34] allotted a village in the Anarudra Viṣaya of *Dakṣiṇa* Tosāli (South Tosāli) to the brāhmaṇa Jālu Bhaṭṭa. Another king of this dynasty Śubhakara I[35] combined two villages in *Uttara* Tosāli (North Tosāli) into one and granted the unit to two hundred brāhmaṇas. Daṇḍī Mahādevī[36] of the same dynasty alienated a village in the Arthani Viṣaya in the Kongoḍa Maṇḍala in *Dakṣiṇa* Kosala in favour of the Bhaṭṭaputra Purushottama. There were so many evidences of the donation of land to the brāhmaṇas by the Bhaumakara rulers during this period.

Epigraphic records of gifts of land to temples are also found. The Hindol plate [37] of the Bhaumakara King Śubhakara II resisters the gift of a village in favour of the god Vidyānātha Bhaṭṭāraka enshrined in the Pulindeśvara temple. Śivakara III's Tālcher Plate[38] executed in Jayasrama Buddhist monastery donated the village Kallani in North Tosāli for the worship of Buddha Bhaṭṭākara at the request of Ranaka Vinitatuṅga.

Certain general procedures were followed in granting land. The declaration of the grant was made known to the headman of the village, brāhmaṇas, royal officials and feaudatories etc. as we see this from the Dhenkanāl plates of Tribhuvana Mahādevī and others.[39] This was done in order to ensure that no injustice was done during the transaction.

Land Tenures

In course of our study of the land grants we came across certain forms of land tenures which prevailed in the case of religious grants. These are (1) *bhūmicchidrapiḍhāna-nyāya*, (2) *nivi-dharma*, and (3) *akṣayanivi-dharma*.

Bhūmicchidrapiḍhāna-nyāya

We find this term in the Śāntigrāma grant of Dandī Mahādevī[40] and the copper-plate charter of Tribhuvana Mahādevī.[41] This term does not find mention in any of the contemporary records outside Orissa. In fact we find the term *bhūmicchidranyāya* in the Kauṭilya's *Arthaśāstra*,[42] the meaning of which may be assigned as Virgin land which was brought under cultivation for the first time.

The term *bhūmicchidrapiḍhāna-nyāya* is translated by H.P. Sastri[43] as leaving holes on earth through which no pen can pass, but this has not been accepted by many scholars. According to D.C. Sircar,[44] the whole term implies that the loss of the lands probably of the donee owing to various causes was to be compensated by making free gifts of some of them. This means that the custom of reclaiming fallow land[45] was prevalent during this period. This view of Dr. Sircar seems to be correct. Generally it was seen that the villages granted under this category were inhabitated by the *tantavāyas* (weaver), *saundhikas* (ventner) and *gokūṭas* (cowherd).

Nivi-dharma

This term appears in the Hindol plate[46] of Śubhakaradeva. According to this, a gift of land was to be maintained perpetually by the donee, but he could make use of the income arising from it. He could not have the right of destroying the perpetuity of the grant by bestowing it on another person.

Akṣayanivi-dharma

This term was found in the Bhauma records also. According to this system the land granted was to be treated as *akṣayanivi* where the original endowment was in no circumstances to be destroyed or diminished.

The rights of the donees under all these terms not only extended over land but also over water and other things that existed on land. One of the remarkable features of the landgrants made in settled areas was the transfer by the donors of not only villages with various kinds of dues but also with weavers, brewers, cowherds and other subjects.[47] Such grants must have reduced these people to semi-serfs, producing surplus for the benefit of brāhmaṇa grantees. In most cases land was given free of all dues for religious purposes. This must have resulted in considerable loss of state revenue.

The result of landgrant to brāhmaṇas in Orissa was the imposition of superior land holders upon ordinary culitivators. It gave power and prestige to priestly grantees. Whatever might be the intentions of the donors, the grants helped to create powerful intermediaries wielding considerable economic and administrative power. Thus the germs of a feudal society was sown during this period. From the inscriptions of this period it is quite evident that the state maintained a regular department for land survey, land measurement and land revenue. To prevent boundary disputes among the villages as well as entry of trespassers, the state had to be vigil. Land survey and land measurement was staffed by *pustapāla*s, who kept careful record of all land transactions.

In the Bhaumakara inscriptions, *māla* is mentioned as a unit of measurement. The Angul copper-plate[48] of Dharma Mahādevī records the donation of ten *māla*s of land. The term *māla* may denote the same measure as *mā* (in south Indian measure) which is 1/20th of a veli.[49] There is in Orissa a land measure called *māna* which is equivalent to 3/5 of an acre. It may be possible that the word *māla* is a scribe's mistake for *māna*. It is found that there was no uniform system of land measure due to the rule of various dynasties.

Agriculture

We can classify the lands in the Bhaumakara period under two groups, viz. *sakheta* (habitable land), and *gulmaka* (forest land). The mention of *gokūṭas* (cowherds) in the records leads us to believe the existence of *sadvāla* (pasture land). Though the bulk of the lands must have been devoted to agriculture, curiously enough the Bhauma records have omitted these lands. Besides there might also have existed *ūsara* (barren) land, as we get the reference to cultivable land which implies the existene of barren lands.

Because of the immigration of a large number of brāhmaṇas from different parts of the country, there came about a steady increase in the cultivable area, as is shown by the copper-plate inscriptions. From the grant of the land in a forest area, it is apparent that jungles were reclaimed and gradually brought under cultivation. Thus we see a steady extension and improvement of cultivation and rural settlement. The pressure of a growing population due to the immigration of the brāhmaṇas, the increasing desire of the brāhmaṇas for material progress and the religious zeal of kings, all served in various ways to bring the fallow land under cultivation.

Orissa had a vast tracts of fertile land. Hiuen-Tsang refers to the fertility of the soil and rich cultivation in Oḍra, Kongoḍa, Kaliṅga and Kosala.[50]

Regarding irrigation we do not find any reference to irrigational projects. But the inscriptions of this period refer to words such as *vāpi*, *tataka*, *sarah*, *puṣkariṇi* etc., which are related to water. It is probable that these places have been utilised for irrigational purpose.

Kaliṅga was well-known for its varieties of rice since the early times. The Hindol plate of the Bhauma King Śubhakara[51] mentions the sowing of paddy (*dhānya*). Besides rice, we get the reference of variety of crops like barley, wheat, sugarcane etc. From the reference to weavers, we may be assured of the existence of cotton cultivation. The cultivation of betal leaf (*tāmbūla*) was also practised. Fruits like mango, banyan, pālm, coconut, bel, palmyra, tamarind etc. were known in Orissa during this period.

Tax and Expenditure

The subjects used to pay land taxes, forest cesses, ferry tolls etc. to the government. Special taxes were imposed on weavers, cowherds, distillers, potters, blacksmiths, goldsmiths and carpenters. Taxes were also collected from *sukheta* (groups of houses), *ghāṭṭa* (landing places for boatmen), *naditarastāna* (ferry place) and *gulmaka* (forest).

The rents from the crown lands collected by the Bhaumakara ruler amounted to 1/6th of the gross produce of the soil. As such land tax was very light. We notice in the Tālcher plate of Śubhakara IV,[52] the mention of *samyuk kara* which may mean prosperity taxes. We come across a term *upari kara* in the Bhauma records which has been identified by Dr. D.C. Sirkar as 'extra cess'.[53] Besides on committing offences, traditional fines were imposed on culprits.

The expenditure of the state included the salary of the officials, the maintenance of the royal family and establishment, worship of deities, charity to ascetics, and reward to scholars. The Bhauma officials received landgrants in lieu of their salaries. It is known from the study that the posts of the officials were usually hereditary.

Medium of Exchange

We have no idea about the medium of exchange during this period. As the Hindol plate of Śubhakara III[54] of the Bhauma dynasty mentioned about *cowrie*, we can presume that the ordinary daily transactions were probably made by *cowries*. *Cowries* cannot be regarded as coins proper, because they did not bear any royal stamp.

Though we have no evidence about the existence of gold coins in the Bhaumakara period, a study of the feudatory kings under the Bhaumas proves the existence of silver coins called *rupyā* in this period. The Tālcher copper grant[55] of the Sulki ruler Kulastambha of the ninth century AD, and the Tālcher plate[56] of the Tuṅga ruler Gayaḍatuṅgadeva of the eleventh century AD, show that a type of coinage known as *rupyā* was in circulation in those days in Orissa. As no such silver coin has been discovered yet, nothing definite can be said about their weight and the metal.

As we have an interesting testimony to the prevalence of cash payments of land revenues in Bhauma charters, we can presume the existence of some sort of silver currency in this period. The exact relation between the silver coins and *cowries* cannot be specified because of insufficient datas.

It seems certain that the barter system existed side by side with the currency.

Weight and Measures

There was no table of weights and measures in the Bhauma copper-plates. The Hindol plate of Śubhakara III discloses *ādhaka* as a measure of rice.[57] According to lexicon *Śabdakalpadruma*, the *ādhaka* is defined as the quarter part of a *droṇa*, in practice 16 or 20 seers.[58]

Crafts and Industries

Although agriculture occupied prominent position in Orissa, we have evidence that several crafts and industries developed during the Bhaumakara period.

The manufacture of textiles appear to have carried on with great success in Orissa. Sculptural remains of many temples of this period show that fine bracaded fabrics were produced in Orissa. R.L. Mitra remarks, that "in neatness, elegance and richness of design and execution, it is in no way inferior to the finest production of the Benares loom of the present-day.[59] Different items of dresses were prepared, e.g. *dhotīs*, *sāḍīs*, *cādara* or scarf, *pāyajāmā*, etc., as known from the sculptures of this period.

In the field of metallurgy Orissa made considerable progress, R.L. Mitra opines that iron was probably obtained from Tālcher, where it is smelted to this day and was of excellent quality.[60] Iron was used especially for building temples. The temples of this period had iron beams in their structure. Iron was used for the manufacture of weapons and armaments such as the battle-axe sword, dagger etc., as evidenced from the sculptures. R.L. Mitra is of the opinion that the dagger or short sword and its varieties seem to have been a great favourite.[61]

Our inscriptions mention the goldsmith (*suvarṇaka*). This is a proof of the large scale use of ornaments made of gold and silver. The sculptures of this period have representations of a variety of ornaments like *kuṇḍala* (ear-ring), *karṇaphūla* (ear-flower), *ratnahāra* (necklace), *candrahāra* (necklace), *kaṭi-bandha* (waist ornament), *bāju kinkiṇi*, (leg and foot ornaments) etc. These precious ornaments were set with pearls and diamonds. Because of the high cost, these ornaments must have been used only by the kings, queens or other royal courtiers. From the designs of the ornaments it can be said that the jewellers were great artists. There was no machinery and hence no stereotyped design was found during this period.

The discovery of large number of copper-plates and bronze images indicate that copper and bronze manufacturing was in a flourishing condition and it must have provided employment to a large number of artisans during this period. After iron, the most useful metal of that period was copper. The skill of engraving letters in the copper-plate was a highly technical art and no doubt, well paid engravers were permanently maintained by the state. The discovery of a large hoard of bronze images from Bānpur was the clear proof of the high standard of bronze casting in those days.

The temples and images belonging to this period testify the skill and volume of the stone work. The Buddhist sculptures of Ratnagiri, Udayagiri, and Lalitagiri hills in the Cuttack district of Orissa are master-pieces of sculptural art. These temples and images were constructed either of reddish granite resembling sand stone or of the free stone.[62] The huge rock cut statues in the Dhenkanāl and Tālcher districts[63] of Orissa show the existence of the craft of creating sculptures out of the parent rock in the ninth and tenth centuries AD. Work in stone must have offered a good vocation to masons, stone-cutters and sculptors.

Pottery was one of the most important industries of that period as we get sculptural representations of pots from the temples belonging to this period. Various other crafts, industries and vocations like, wood work, ivory work, perfumery, oil industry, boat making, tanning, salt works, etc. existed during this period.

There is nothing to show that the state itself played an important part in the industrial production. Most of the crafts and industries seem to have been carried on by individual families. One of the reasons behind the success in various industries is probably the esteem in which the artisans were held.

Trade and Commerce

The sources of our internal and external trade include inscriptions and accounts of Hiuen-Tsang and other foreign travellers, mostly comprised Arabians.

Internal Trade

There used to be probably a market servicing a number of villages as is suggested by reference to a market *hāṭṭah* in an inscription from Jājpur assigned to the seventh/eighth century AD.[64] Here villagers sold a portion of their produce or purchased necessary articles. Sometimes markets have developed near a temple to meet the needs of pilgrims coming from distant places. Certain places become important because of commercial activities. A copper-plate grant of the Bhañja King Neṭṭabhañja assigned to the eighth century AD informs us that Angulaka (present-day Angul in Dhenkanāl district of Orissa) was made prosperous by the merchants community, who sold commodities of all descriptions on a large scale.[65]

The articles of internal trade included all sorts of commodities. Fragrant substances, conch-shells, wood, ornaments, bronze goods, betel leaves, sugar, cloth, earthern vessels, fish, foodgrains, vegetable, milk, oil, fruits etc. were some of the articles of trade. Frequent references to brewers in grants of villages to the donees show that liquor was also an article of local trade.[66] Elephant and diamonds formed articles of long distant trade.

Elephants and carts pulled by bullocks were used for transportation of goods to different places. The Arabian geographers[67] mentioned that extremely large elephants were found in Orissa. The rivers like Vaitaraṇī, Brāhmaṇī, Mahānadī and their tributaries served as arteries of water borne trade. The epigraphic references to the grant of right over landing places on the bank of river (*ghāṭa*), ferry places (*nadī-tarasthāna*) suggest the use of boats on a large scale.

External Trade

From very early times Orissa seems to have commercial relations with different countries in the world. Kaliṅga had commercial intercourse with the islands of Bāli, Jāvā, Sumātrā, Bornes, Mālāya and other neighbouring countries. Hiuen-Tsang[68] describes a port city called Chelita-lo (Charitra), situated on the sea coast of the Oḍra *deśa*, identified with Puri by Prof. R.D. Banerji.[69] According to the pilgrim this city was a thoroughfare and resting place for sea going traders. Another important and prosperous port in Orissa was Pālur.[70] R.C. Majumdar[71] is of the opinion that a direct voyage to the east was made from the port of Pālur. According to U.N.

Ghosal[72] the most important event in the economic history of Eastern and Southern Asia during the sixth century AD, was an inter-oceanic trade reaching from China through Indonesia and the east coast of India up to Ceylon.

It is very likely, that Orissa used to carry on Oceanic trade with China during the eighth-ninth century AD. This observation finds corroboration from the visit of Prajñā from Orissa to China during the reign of a Bhauma monarch Śivakara I. We know that one of the Bhauma kings had copied with his own hand the *Gaṇḍavyūha*, a *Mahāyāna* text and presented it to the emperor of China. This cultural relation presupposes commercial relation.[73] The fact is further proved by the discovery of a copper (Chinese) coin attributable to the eighth century AD found from Sirpur during the excavation.[74] From the accounts of Arab travellers it is clear that brisk maritime trade was being carried on with the foreign countries. They mentioned about a port Nubin in Orissan coast, which is unfortuantely not identified. The provisions and corn of Sarandib came from this town.[75] Sarandib is identified with Suvarṇadvīpa or modern Sumātrā.[76]

The items of export were cloth, various types of cereals, rice, wheat, barely, salt, incense, timber, ivory, conch-shells, stone, iron products, diamonds, elephants etc. This information has been given by the contemporary literature and records of the foreign visitors.

The articles of imports might be silver and copper of Ceylon, cloves and skikenard of Jāvā and Sumātrā, the silk from China etc. We have very little information about the import trade as the contemporary literature and epigraphic records were silent about this.

According to the testimony of Sulaiman[77] India had few horses during the eighth-ninth century AD. The best breed of horses known to India at that period came from Western and Central Asia. We may believe that an extensive and valuable export trade in horses was carried on with India by the countries on her Western frontier. As we have reference to cavalry, in the Bhauma records and sculptural depiction of the same in the temples of that period, we believe that horses might have come to Orissa from Western and Central Asia. Therefore it is probable that Orissa had trade relations with states in Central and Western Asia during this period.

CONTEMPORARY INDIA'S ECONOMIC CONDITION

The comparison between the economic condition of Bengal and Orissa as a unit and that of India can be made if we study in brief about various important economic aspects of Indian society of the period from eighth to twelfth century AD.

Agriculture

From the records of this period we have evidences of advanced state of agriculture prevailing in most parts of India. *Abhidhānaratnamālā*[78] mentions about a large variety of cereals and other foodgrains, like paddy, wheat, barely, pulses, sugarcane etc. in different parts of India. It also mentioned about the people's knowledge of scientific agriculture. It further says that different kinds of fields were selected for different classes of crops. The fields were classified according to their qualities, namely, those which were fertile, those unfit for cultivation, those under cultivation, those lying fallow, and those with a saline soil. *Upamiti-bhāvaprapañcakathā*,[79] in a description of the winter season mentions that machines (*yantra*) were used for crushing big sugarcanes. We also get references about rich cultivation and fertility of soil from the writings of Arab travellers to India.

From the traditions we know that the Cola king's of this period constructed the famous anicuts across the Kāverī river in Tanjore district, which were renovated in much later times by the British Government.

From the indigenous and foreign sources we get the picture of some principal agricultural regions. Magadha was famous for good quality of rice, Kashmir was notable for good variety of grapes and other fruits, Mālābār was famous for pepper, the Gulf of Cāmbay was famous for bamboo, the Mālāya hills famous for sandal wood and Gujarat for cotton.

Village and City

A large scale distribution of grants and assignments by different royal dynasties must have led to the creation of larger or smaller estates comprising numbers of villages. The royal grants transferred the king's dues and rights in favour of the donees.

In the south, the village communities maintained their corporate organisation with full vigour. We see there was a vigourous growth of city-life during this period. We have descriptions of various cities by contemporary Indian and foreign writers.

Industry and Crafts

The reocrds of this period mention a great variety and different qualities of textiles such as woollen, and hampen yarns, garments made of silk and of Ranku deer's hair and of sheep's and goat's wool, cotton textile of unique fineness, manufactured in Bengal. This description has given enough idea about the advanced state of textile industry during this period. Cola kingdom was famous for ivory works. Gujarat and Cāmbay region produced large number of dressed skins and beautiful leather mats embroidered with gold and silver wire.

The working of metals in a large scale was also mentioned. The list of metals which are mentioned in the contemporary literature as well as epigraphic records includes copper, brass, iron, lead, tin, silver and gold. *Abhidhānaratnamālā*[80] mentions that Surāṣṭra was famous for its bell metal (brass), while Vaṅga was well-known for its tin industry. Various texts of this period mention the list of jewellery. *Agni Purāṇa* mentions no less than thirtythree kinds of gems and analyses the good qualities of diamond, emerald, ruby, pearls and *vaidūrya.* The vast scale and super quality of the stone sculpture of this period are illustrated by the numerous examples of stone images and temples scattered all over the country.

The general rule governing the economic activities was stated by Medhātithi.[81] He says that the vaiśya is to perform the occupations of agriculture, money lending, trade and cattle breeding. Except in times of distress, no caste other than vaiśya was allowed to take up the activities of vaiśya. The king had the right to punish the culprit.

Medhātithi[82] further says that handicraft was regarded as a very low occupation.

Trade

It is surprising to note that almost all the records of this period are silent about the extent and direction of India's internal trade. Scattered references indicate that India's trade with the outside world was carried on both by land and sea. By this time the Arab merchants from Southern Arabia had built up trade links with India.

From the accounts of the Arab writers, we get a knowledge about the foreign trade and the sea ports through which trade was going on with foreign countries. The list of Indian sea ports mentioned by them include Sindh, near the mouth of river Indus, Kāmbay on the Gujarat coast, Thānā, Sopāra and Sindān (near Bombay), Quilon on the Mālābār coast.[83]

Exports

Ibn Khordādhba,[84] the Arabian writer mentions that Indian exports of agricultural and forest products include diverse species of aloe-wood, sandal wood, camphor, nutmeg, elove pink, cubele, cocoanut, vegetable stuffs, and velvety cotton. It appears that costus from the Himālayan region, Indigo from Gujarat as well as camphor and rattan from Māyāla and Sumātrā were brought to the ports of Sindh for export. Teak from western India, pepper from Sindan and sandals from Cāmbay were exported. Other items of export coming from south India included sandal wood, pepper, cardamom and various perfume bearing plants.[85]

Kāmarūpa, according to Abu Zaid, produced a variety of aloe-wood called *kāmarūbī* which was valued at that time at 200 Arabian *dīnāra*s per mound. Cotton textiles of unique fineness were manufactured in Bengal during this period and exported to other places outside India.

Medhātithi[86] mentions that precious stones and pearls from south India, horses from west, elephants from east as well as saffron, silk and woollen from Kashmir were exported to foreign lands. Arab writers Sulaiman and Masudi[87] mentioned that horns of rhinoceros were exported from the kingdom of Rahma, identified as Bengal, to China for being made into fashionable and costly girdles.

As regards mineral products, antimony (*srotonjana*), rock salt (*saindhava lavaṇa*), and beryl (*vaidūrya*) were exported. Sulaiman and Masudi[88] mentioned that gold and silver found in the kingdom of Gudjra, identified as Kanauj under the Gurjara-Pratihāras and in Rahna (Bengal) were among the exported items.

Imports

According to Sulaiman[89] and Ibn al Fakih, India imported the best breed of horses from Western and Central Asia as India had very few good quality horses. Imports of wine from Kapisa is hinted in *Abhidhānaratnamālā*.[90] The Arab writer Ibn[91] mentions the import of dates from Basra (in the Gulf region). From the phrase of *Chināmsuka*, meaning Chinese silk in the literatures of this period, we are sure that silk was brought to India from China. Cloves, spikenard and other fine spices were brought into Mālābār from Jāvā and Sumātrā, copper and gold also came to India from Sumātrā.

Organisation of Industry and Trade

We learn from Medhātithi[92] that both industrial and mercantile guilds functioned during this time. He defines the guild (*śreṇī*) as consisting of people following common professions, such as tradesman, artisans, moneylenders, coach-drivers, and many others. He further mentions another mercantile organisation called *saṁgha*, which consisted of persons following the same pursuit, though belonging to different castes (*jāti*) and regions (*deśa*). The mercantile *saṁgha* unlike the guild, was an association of traders comprising different castes and inhabiting different regions.

The guilds as well as the *saṁgha*s had the right of making bye-laws, that were binding on their merchants. Besides *śreṇī* and *saṁgha* there were associations of labourers and of capitalists as well.

We have the informations about the guilds of weavers, potters, gardeners, and artisans. The executive of these guilds consisted sometimes of many headmen and sometimes even single headman. In accordance with the old *Smṛti* rule the guild arranged for distribution of different tasks among its members.

According to Medhātithi precious stones and pearls of south India, horses of west, elephants in the east and saffron, silk and wools of Kashmir were royal monopolies and private trading in them was punishable.

In south India the village assemblies called *sabhā* and *ur* often acted as bankers and public trustees during our period.

It is noteworthy that the relation between capital and labour was systematically laid down by the laws of that period. There were labour laws which dealt with wages, compensation and liabilities.

We may conclude that there was development in every economic activity. In agriculture, industry and trade India made a great headway during this period. This proves beyond doubt that India had a high level of economic prosperity during this period.

Notes

1. *EI*, II, p. 357.
2. Pāṭaliputra and Kapila in the records of Dharmapāla and Mudgagiri in the records of Devapāla and Nārāyaṇapāla.
3. *Pāla Inscription*, Nos. 23, 31, 39.
4. *EI*, XV, p. 130.
5. *EI*, XVIII, p. 63.
6. U.N. Ghosal, *Agrarian System in Ancient India* (1930), p. 41.
7. U.N. Ghosal, *The Hindu Revenue System* (1929), pp. 244-46.
8. B.C. Sen, *Some Historical Aspects of the Inscriptions of Bengal*, p. 568.
9. N.G. Majumdar, *Inscriptions of Bengal*, Vol, III, pp. 130, 147.
10. *MASB*, I, pp. 88, 90.
11. U.N. Ghosal, *The Agrarian System in Ancient India,* p. 60.
12. *IHQ*, VI, p. 56, 59, 60.
13. *EI*, XV, p. 307, 311.
14. N.C. Majumdar, *Inscriptions of Bengal*, II, p. 97.

15. *IA*, 1910, pp. 214-16.
16. R.C. Majumdar (ed.), *History of Bengal*, p. 653.
17. *EI*, XXII p. 155,158.
18. *IB*, p. 5.
19. *Ibid.*, p. 21.
20. Kumauli CP — *Gauḍa-Lekha-Mālā* in Bengali by A.K. Maitreya.
21. Nidharpur CP.
22. *IB*, p. 128.
23. P.C. Chakravarti, *The Art of War in Ancient India*, pp. 163-64.
24. N.K. Bhattasali, *Catalogue of sculptures in the Dacca Museum*, p. XVIII.
25. *Ibid.*, p. XXXV, XXXVI.
26. R.C. Majumdar (ed.), *History of Bengal*, p. 658.
27. *EI*, XV, 130 ff.
28. *IB*, pp. 45-46.
29. *EI*, IV, p. 254.
30. Beal Records II, p. 195.
31. *EI*, II, p. 345.
32. Beal Records II, 204 ff.
33. B.C. Sen, *Historical Aspects of the Inscriptions of Bengal*, p. 571.
34. *JBORS*, XIV, pp. 292-306.
35. *EI*, XV, pp. 1-8.
36. *EI*, VI, pp. 140-42.
37. *JBORS*, XVI, pp. 69-83.
38. B. Mishra, *op. cit.* pp. 40-50.
39. *EI*, XIX, p. 137, *JBORS*, II pp. 426-27.
40. *EI*, XXIX, Part IV, p. 39.
41. *JBORS*, II, p. 423.
42. *Arthaśāstra*, II, pp. 49, 50.
43. *JBORS*, II, p. 427.
44. *JBORS*, XVI, p. 81.
45. *EI*, XXIX, Part IV, p. 86.
46. *Ibid.*
47. Dhenkanal plate of Tribhuvanadevi, *JBORS* II, pp. 426-27.

48. *JAS*, XVII, No. 3, p. 246.
49. *EI*, VII, No. 20, p. 143.
50. Beal, *Buddhist Records* II, pp. 204-09.
51. *JBORS*, XVI, p. 83.
52. B. Mishra, *Orissa Under the Bhauma Kings*, p. 19.
53. D.C. Sircar, *Select Inscriptions* I, p. 266.
54. B. Mishra, *Orissa Under the Bhuma Kings*, p. 15.
55. *EI*, XII, No. 20, p. 158.
56. *JASB*, NS, XII, p. 294.
57. *Op. cit.* p. 19.
58. *Śabdakalpadruma*, Vol. I, p. 249.
59. R.L. Mitra, *Antiquities of Orissa*, I, p. 80.
60. *Ibid.*, p. 36
61. *Ibid.*, p. 123.
62. N.K. Sahu (ed.), *A History of Orissa*, Vol. II, p. 267.
63. *OHRJ*, III, No. 2, p. 77.
64. *EI*, XXVIII, Part IV, p. 183.
65. *JBORS*, XVII, p. 114.
66. *JBORS*, XVIII, pp. 81-83.
67. *Hudud-al-Alam*, p. 87.
68. T. Walters, *Travels in India* II, pp. 193 ff.
69. R.D. Banerji, *History of Orissa*, I, p. 138.
70. McCrindle (tr.), *Ancient India as described by Ptolemy*, pp. 22, 63.
71. R.C. Majumdar, *Ancient Indian Colonies in the Far East*, II, p. 7.
72. R.C. Majumdar (ed.), *Classical Age*, p. 598.
73. A.P. Sah, *Life in Medieval Orissa*, p. 110.
74. *OHRJ*, No. 2, p. 104.
75. *Hudud-al-Alam*, p. 86.
76. K.C. Panigrahi, *History of Orissa*, p. 93.
77. R.C. Majumdar (ed.), *Age of Imperial Kanauj*, pp. 404, 405.
78. *Ibid.*, p. 399.
79. *Ibid.*, p. 400.

80. *Ibid.*, p. 401.
81. *Ibid.*, p. 405.
82. *Ibid.*
83. Elliot and Dowson. (ed.), *History of India as told by its own historians*, I pp. 15, 37, 441.
84. *Ibid.*
85. R.C. Majumdar (ed.), *Age of Imperial Kanauj*, p. 402.
86. *Ibid.*, p. 403.
87. *Ibid.*
88. *Ibid.*
89. *Ibid.*, p. 404.
90. *Ibid.*
91. *Ibid.*
92. *Ibid.*, p. 405.

6

Conclusion

In the preceding pages, we have discussed about the religious, social as well as political history of Bengal and Orissa from eighth to twelfth century AD. Let us conclude this study with some of the important findings of the work.

The period from eighth to twelfth century AD was a transitional one from ancient to medieval perriod. It was the period when feudalism was raising its head in both Bengal and Orissa. There was a total transformation in the religious, social and economic relations.

The Pālas in Bengal and the Bhaumakaras in Orissa gave political stability in their respective kingdoms ending a state of anarchy and uncertainty. Their long rule gave geographical unity to their respective regions.

It is a fact that the Pālas of Bengal and the Bhaumakaras of Orissa had many things in common. They almost simultaneously began their rules and ruled for a long period though the Pālas ruled longer than the Bhaumakaras. Most of the rulers of both the dynasties were great devotees of Lord Buddha and made great efforts for the furtherance of their faith. They were not bigots as they simultaneously gave unequivocal support to other religious sects along with Buddhism.

During this period all the major religious beliefs like Buddhism,

Śaivism and Vaiṣṇavism seem to have synthesized into a cosmopolitan form of religion loosing their separate entities. The process of assimilation between Brāhmaṇism and Buddhism started during this period as we see Buddha was accepted as an *avatāra* (incarnation) of Viṣṇu by the brāhamaṇas and on the other hand Buddhism adopted many of the Brāhmaṇic rituals into its fold. The cult of Śakti was engulfing all these major religious faiths. This period saw the greatest transformation of Buddhism from Mahāyānism to Tāntrism mostly due to the impact of the Śakti cult. Countless anonymous *Siddācārya*s changed the basic ideals of Buddhism and infused new blood to its body. It was a landmark in the career of Buddhism that Mahāyānism changed into Tāntrism which has three different *yāna*s or systems, i.e., *Vajrayāna*, *Kālacakrayāna* and *Sahajayāna*. Among them *Vajrayāna* is best expressive of the ritualistic and doctrinal characteristics of the Tāntric from the Buddhism.

We find a lot of Tāntric images from Bengal and Orissa belonging to the period of our study which prove beyond doubt the success of *Tantrayāna* Buddhism. Due to the patronage of the rulers of Bengal and Orissa of this period a large number of Buddhist centres sprang up which attracted scholars not only from India but also from foreign countries like China, Tibet and Nepal. This religious interaction paved the way for cultural, social and economic relations with foreign countries.

It is significant to note that although most of the kings of Bengal and Orissa of this period were Buddhists, they had great respect for other religious faiths. In fact so far as landgrants of these two dynasties of our period are concerned, the maximum number of donees were adherents of Brāhmaṇism. Thus the rulers followed the tradition of religious catholicity which resulted in the socio-cultural unity of the people in spite of professing different religious faiths. In the social hierarchy the brāhmaṇas stood on top. Though they were supposed to engage themselves in learning, rituals and worship, they sometimes do certain other professions, usually not prescribed to them. In both Orissa and Bengal brāhmaṇas occupied the most important position and they got various landgrants from the ruling families of the period of our study. We have seen that in this period the ruling families invited many brāhmaṇa families to Orissa and Bengal from Madhyadeśa, Śrāvastī and other northern states.

In Orissa next to the brāhmaṇas, the kṣatriyas enjoyed a high social status. It is noteworthy that in Bengal we find no kṣatriya caste unlike in other areas. Kāyasthas and Karanas, occupied also a high position in the society. They not only wrote documents but also held high responsible posts in the state adminstration.

The vaiśyas, though socially occupied a position next to brāhmaṇas, kṣatriyas and kāyastha, control the economic activity of the people, thus occupying an important position in the society.

The society did not rigidly follow the rules of caste system prescribed to it in the *Dharmaśāstra*s.

The rulers of this period tried to maintain the caste system based on *Darmaśāstra*s. In the Neulpur plate of Śubhakaradeva I, it is mentioned that Kṣemaṅkaradeva, the first king of the Bhaumakara dynasty in Orissa established four order (castes) in their proper duties. As already stated Kṣemaṅkara was a devout Buddhist. Thus it is strange to note that a king who professed Buddhism, (which opposes caste system), was establishing the caste system in order. It happened probably due to the control of the brāhmaṇas over the state administration. As the ruling house namely the Bhaumakaras had aboriginal origin, outside the periphery of the Brāhmaṇical social system, the rulers tried to satisfy the brāhmaṇas in order to get legitimacy to their rule from the brāhmaṇas.

The position of women in society was very high. It is very significant to note that five widowed queens and a daughter of the ruling monarchs of the Bhaumakara dynasty in Orissa ruled with full regal status. This is an unprecendented event in Indian history. This might be possible due to the influence of Buddhist doctrine of giving equal status to women. We do not find such example except a few cases, in other parts of India.

The practice of *satī* and concubinage was very rare in Bengal and Orissa during the period of our study. The system of *purdāh* (veil) was unknown to Bengal and Orissan society.

The contemporary *Dharma-Sūtra*s allowed women very few legal rights and privileges.

In Bengal we come across with certain descriptions in the contemporary literature from which we can conclude that there was a low standard of sexual morality during this period due to excess wealth, luxury and extravagance. This immorality was responsible for certain evil customs like keeping female slaves and *devadāsī* system (keeping women dancers in temples). Another factor contributing to this low standard of sexual morality was the growth of Tantrism in both Buddhism and Brāhmaṇism.

In the field of education and learning it was the glorious period in the region of our study. For the growth of education Buddhism had played a great and significant role. The Buddhist monasteries functioned as centres of education and learning. Scholars from different parts of the country and outside the country came to study and thus paved the way for great cultural and commercial interaction among our area of study and other countries.

Though Sanskrit language was used in most of the inscriptions and official records, the language of Bengali and Oriyā began to develop gradually in Bengal and Orissa respectively during this period.

When we compare the society during the eighth to twelfth century AD in Bengal and Orissa to that of other areas of India (outside the area of our study) we find many things in common with very rare differences.

Like in Bengal and Orissa, the brāhmaṇas occupied the highest position in the social hiararchy throughout India. The brāhmaṇas of Andhra, Orissa, Tamil Nadu and Punjab were regarded as degraded brāhmaṇas. We find that brāhmaṇas took to different other professions, not prescribed by *Śāstra*s (religious scriptures) due to forcible circumstances. The kṣatriyas unlike in Bengal and Orissa were distinctively split up into two classes, e.g. Rājpūts (the kings and rulers), and ordinary kṣatriyas (cultivators and landholders). We see in most parts of India that the *varṇa* system (caste system), prescribed by *Śāstra*s was not strictly followed during this period. Though the Kāyastha or Karana caste was regarded as śūdras due to their unauspicious origin, in most of the areas of India, like in Bengal and Bihar, they were given a high status in society because of their function as writer of inscriptions. The

Kāyastha caste had not been split up, as we find today. The contemporary *Dharmaśāstras* recognised the śūdra's right to personal freedom though a śūdra was not entitled to initiation.

An interesting point to mark in this period outside Bengal and Orissa was that the heretical sects like Buddhists, Pāśupatas and Lokāyatikas were kept under the untouchable category probably because of their opposition to the caste-system.

As regards the position of women in society, we see that unlike in Bengal and Orissa, in other parts of India there was restriction on queens and lady members of the royal family to appear in the court. It is interesting to note that a list of duties and rights for the prostitutes were laid down by the *Purāṇas* of this period. Unlike in Bengal and Orissa particularly Orissa where we find woman ruling over during this period, in other parts of India we see that women had no freedom of action on the subjects like virtue, wealth and pleasure.

The economic condition of the people of Bengal and Orissa was satisfactory. We observe that the kings, queens and other royal and rich persons of this period in Bengal and Orissa donated lands to various secular as well as religious institutions and to individuals particularly brāhamaṇas and Buddhists. The donee was given the right of collecting regular revenue together with extra revenues. We see that the brāhmaṇa donees far outnumbered the secular assignees though most of the rulers of this period in the area of our study were Buddhists.

This period witnessed a great increase of cultivation in Bengal and Orissa. The pressure of a growing population, the growing desire of the priests for material prosperity, the religious zeal of the kings — all were responsible for the extension of agricultural lands.

Various kinds of crops like rice, barley, wheat, sugarcane, cotton, oilseeds and betel leaf were produced in abundance in this area. Rice of Kaliṅga and cotton of Bengal were very famous outside this area.

In other parts of India we observe that people were acquianted with the scientific way of agriculture. Machines were used for crushing different food crops. There were good irrigation systems in south India during this period. Different areas were famous for different crops like Magadha for rice, Kashmir for grapes, Mālābār for pepper, Mālāya area for sandalwood and Gujarat for cotton.

When we compare the agricultural knowledge of Bengal and Orissa with that of other parts of India, we see that the agriculture of other parts of India was more scientific.

Another important observation is that there was an increase of urban centres not only in Bengal and Orissa but also in other parts of India due to the prosperity in trade and commerce, education and learning and political stability.

A number of crafts and industries such as weaving, dyeing, metal work, jewellery, ivory work, wood work, stone work, pottery, tanning and many others were practised both in Bengal and Orissa. Cotton textiles of unique fineness were manufactured in the region of our study. As we find a large number of copper-plates and a number of life sized Buddhist status in Bengal and Orissa, we can safely say that the braziers and masons of this area were skilful artists.

In other areas of India we have references of various crafts and industries. Saurāṣṭra was famous for brass industry, Cola kingdom was famous for ivory works and Gujarat and Cāmbay were famous for leather industry. There was overall prosperity in the stone industry throughout India.

The general rule governing the economic activities was that the vaiśya was to perform the occupations of agriculture, moneylending, trade and cattle breeding. In normal times this rule was expected to be followed and king had been given the right to punish the culprit of violating this rule.

It was the age of great prosperity in maritime trade and commerce. Both Bengal and Orissa had trade contacts with Mālāya, Jāvā, Sumātrā, Sri Lanka (Ceylone), China and with some middle east countries. External trade was carried on through different ports like Charitra (Purī), Pālur, Tāmralipti etc. Articles of import included silver, spices and silk and important articles of export were cereals, incense, timber, ivory, diamonds and elephants.

There were many ports found all over India during this period. Important among these were Sindh, in the mouth of Indus, Kāmbay on Gujarat Coast, Thānā, Sopāra and Sindān in Mahārāṣṭra and Quilon on the Mālābār Coast. Custus of the Himālayan region, Indigo of Gujarat, sandal wood, pepper, cardamom etc. of South India and aloe-wood of Kāmarūpa were exported to foreign countries. The articles of import included horses, wine, dates, cloves, gold and copper.

We do not find any mercantile or industrial guilds in Bengal and Orissa during the period of our review. But in other parts of India there were guilds, consisting of people following common professions such as tradesmen and artisans. Another mercantile organisation, found mention in the contemporary literature, was *saṁgha* (different from Buddhist *saṁgha*), which was an association of traders comprising different castes and inhabiting different regions. These organisations had their own laws, binding on their merchants. Besides these organisations, there were associations of labourers and capitalists as well. In South India the village assemblies called *sabhā* and *ur* acted as bankers.

In most of the parts of India, we see that there was systematic growth of class consciousness among labourers and capitalists and each one was conscious of ones rights. There were many labour laws passed by the different states which dealt with wages, compensation and liabilities.

In Bengal and Orissa we do not find any evidence of large scale issuing of coins by the rulers of our period of review. From the discovery of a few copper and silver coins in Bengal (Pahārpur), it appears that an attempt was made to introduce minted currency by the Pāla rulers. But from the debased character of these coins it seems that the attempt was faint hearted one and soon it was abandoned. We see that *cowrie* shells were very much used in Bengal and Orissa during this period. Thus *cowries* might be utilised as a medium of exchange during this period.

As we see that gold coins were profusely used in neighbouring Kāmarūpa during this period, it is strange to see no gold coin from the powerful Pālas of Bengal.

Another important development of this age was the growth of feudalism in the region of our review. The feudal economy of this period had the following prominent features. Firstly there was the growth of individual ownership of land at the cost of royal communal ownership. Secondly the peasant class was subjected to various disabilities through sub-infeudation and imposition of non-customary taxes etc. There came into existence of self-sufficient economy revealed by less frequent use of coins.

Though the process of feudalisation of the administrative machinery in Orissa started from as early as the fifth century AD, it became widespread during the Bhaumakara period. The epigraphic evidences testify to the fact that the administration was decentralised in the form of creation of many feudatory states. Extensive landgrants to brāhmaṇas in lieu of cash payments testify to the inability of the rulers to establish centralised depotism. This happened possibly partly due to the paucity of metallic currency and partly owing to religious considerations. The lands assigned to the brāhmaṇas and to the Buddhist monasteries were actually cultivated by a class of cultivators who had no private land of their own but had owned agricultural implements for cultivation. Thus a class of intermediaries rose who had usufructuary rights over properties. The hereditary peasant families cultivated lands with their own agricultural implements and labour and getting very less quantity of the produce.

This period also witnessed the opening up of the gates of the uncultivated lands in the jungles by these new landed aristocrats. The mobility in the population also is seen during this period which brought uncultivable pasture and forest lands under cultivation.

We may now conclude with the observation that though this period was the most glorious period in the history of Buddhism in the region of our review, still this period sowed the seeds of disintigration of this religion. Buddhism's adaptation of various rituals and controversy over the sexual liberty, given in *tāntrik* Buddhism, made people antagonised aganist Buddhism. The Buddhist monks did have as much influence on the people as compared to the brāhmaṇas. As more and more land was granted to the brāhmaṇas, they became rich which in the other way made them very influential. The brāhmaṇas very shrewdly adjusted to the changing socio-economic patterns, which was not found in the case of

Buddhists, as a result the process of declining of Buddhism started during this period.

The contribution of Buddhism to the field of education and learning was great about which we have already discussed earlier. India's contact with foreign countries was speeded up due to the exchange of religious ideas particularly Buddhist principles among India and other countries. Trade and commerce in Bengal and Orissa showed a significant growth due to Buddhism.

Thus we may now conclude with the remark that Buddhism played a significant role in the sphere of society and economic conditions of Bengal and Orissa, about which we have discussed in the preceding pages.

Appendix

A. (I) Epigraphic records of the Pālas of Bengal

S. No.	*Locality*	*Material*	*Name of the King*	*Reference*
1.	Bodh Gayā	stone	Dharmapāla	*JASB*, N.S., IV, 101
2.	Khālimpur	CP	Dharmapāla	*EI*, IV, 243
3.	Nālandā	stone	Dharmapāla	Nālandā, 85
4.	Nālandā	CP	Dharmapāla	*EI*, XXIII, 290
5.	Nālandā	Metal	Devapāla	Nālandā, 87
6.	Kurkihār	Image	Devapāla	*JBORS*, XXVI, 251
7.	Hilsā	Image	Devapāla	*JBORS*, X, 33
8.	Monghyr	CP	Devapāla	*EI*, XVIII, 304
9.	Nālandā	CP	Devapāla	*EI*, XVII, 318
10.	Ghosrāwa	stone	Devapāla	*IA*, XVII, 307
11.	Nālandā	Votive	Devapāla	Nālandā, 88
12.	Asutosa Museum	stone	Devapāla	*ARIE*, 1949-50, 8
13.	Nālandā	Image	Devapāla	Nālandā, 88
14.	Mirjāpur VP	CP	Surapāla	*JAS*, XIII, 1971, 201 ff.
15.	Bihār	Image	Vigrahapāla I	*JASB*, N.S. IV, 108
16.	Sārnath	Image	Vigrahapāla I	*ASI*, 1907-08,75

S. No.	*Locality*	*Material*	*Name of the King*	*Reference*
17.	Rajauna	stone	Vigrahapāla I	*IHQ*, XXIX, 301
18.	Gayā	Temple	Nārāyāṇapāla	*EI*, XXXV, 225
19.	Indian Museum, Calcutta	stone	Nārāyāṇapāla	*PB*, 61-62
20.	Bhāgalpur	CP	Nārāyāṇapāla	*IA*, XV, 304
21.	Bihār	Image	Nārāyāṇapāla	*IA*, XLVII, 110
22.	Bādāl	Pillar	Nārāyāṇapāla	*EI*, II, 160
23.	Bhārata Kalā Bhavan	CP	Rājyapāla	*Chavi*, II, 222-29
24.	Monghyr	stone	Rājyapāla	*Patna University Journal*, I, I p. 49
25.	Nālandā	Pillar	Rājyapāla	*IA*, XLVII, III
26.	Kurkihār	Image	Rājyapāla	*JBORS*, XXVI, pp. 246-50
27.	Bhāturiyā	stone	Rājyapāla	*EI*, XXXIII, 150
28.	Nālandā	Image	Gopāla II	*JASB*, N.S. IV, 105
29.	Mandhuk (Tipperā)	—	Gopāla II	*IHQ*, XXVIII, 55
30.	Jājilpārā	CP	Gopāla II	*JAS*, XVII, 137
31.	Bodh Gayā	Image	Gopāla II	*JASB*, N.S. IV, 105
32.	Kurkihār (3 plates)	Image	Vigrahapāla II	*JBORS*, XXVI pp.36, 37, 239, 240
33.	Sārnāth	Image	Mahipāla I	*IA*, XIV, 139
34.	Bāghaurā	Image	Mahipāla I	*EI*, XVII, 335
35.	Nārāyāṇapur	Image	Mahipāla I	*IC*, IX, 121
36.	Belwā	CP	Mahipāla I	*EI*, XXIX, 1
37.	Bangarh	CP	Mahipāla I	*EI*, XIV, 329
38.	Nālandā	Image	Mahipāla I	*JASB*, N.S. IV, 106

S. No.	Locality	Material	Name of the King	Reference
39.	Bodh Gayā	Image	Mahipāla I	*PB*, 75
40.	Kurkihār	Image	Mahipāla I	*JBORS*, XXVI, 245
41.	Imādpur	Image	Mahipāla I	*IA*, XIV, 165
42.	Tetrāwan	Image	Mahipāla I	*ASC*, I, 39, III, 123 No. 11
43.	Gayā (2 plates)	Temple	Nayapāla	*EI*, XXXVI, 84, 86
44.	Vālgudār	Image	Nayapāla	*EI*, XXXVIII, 137
45.	Gayā	Temple	Vigrahapāla III	*EI*, XXXVI, 89
46.	Āmgāchhi	CP	Vigrahapāla III	*EI*, XV, 293
47.	Bihar	Image	Vigrahapāla III	*PB*, 112
48.	Bangāon	CP	Vigrahapāla III	*IHQ*, XXVIII, 54
49.	Naulāgarh	Image	Vigrahapāla II or III	*JBRS* XXXVII, 3
50.	Belwā	CP	Vigrahapāla III	*EI*, XXIX, 9
51.	Tetrāwān	Image	Rāmapāla	*JASL*, XVII, 117
52.	Monghyr	Stone	Rāmapāla	*ARIE*, 1949-50, p. 8
53.	Ārmā	Image	Rāmapāla	*ARIE*, 1960-61, p. 17
54.	Monghyr	Stone	Rāmapāla	*ARIE*, 1949-50, p.8
55.	Chandiman	Image	Rāmapāla	*PB*, 93-94
56.	National Museum, Delhi	—	Rāmapāla	*Indo-Asian Culture*, Jan., 1969 p. 61
57.	Asutosh Museum	Stone	Rāmapāla	*ARIE*, 1949-50, p. 8
58.	Rajibpur	Image	Gopāla II or III	*IHQ*, XVII, 217
59.	Nimdighi	Stone	Gopāla II or III	*IHQ*, XVII, 217
60.	Nongadh	Image	Madanapāla	*EI*, XXXVI, 41
61.	Vālgudār	Image	Madanapāla	*EI*, XXVIII, 145
62.	Bihar	Image	Madanapāla	*ASC*, III, 124 No. 6

63.	Mānahāli	CP	Madanapāla	*JASB*, LXIX, 68
64.	Jaynagar	Image	Madanapāla	*ASC*, III, 125
65.	Ārmā	Pillar	Madanapāla	*EI*, XXXVI, 42
66.	Gayā	Stone	Govindapāla	*PB*, 109
67.	Jayanagar	Image	Pālapāla	*JBORS*, XIV, 496

(II) Inscriptions of the Contemporary Ruling Families

S. No	*Locality*	*Material*	*Name of the ruler*	*References*
1.	Lāl	Image	Yasahpāla	*Indian Archeology*, 1953-54, p. 14
2.	Mahisantosh	Image	Mahendrapāla	*EI*, XXXVII, pp. 204-8
3.	Asiatic Society	CP	Bhavadeva	*JAS* (L), XVII, (1951), 83
4.	Chittagong	CP	Kāntideva	*EI*, XXVI, p. 333
5.	Paśсimbhāg	CP	Śrīcandra	*Indian Museum Bulletin*, Jan., 1967, p. 7
6.	Madanpur	CP	Śrīcandra	*EI*, XXVIII p.51
7.	Rāmpāl	CP	Śrīcandra	*EI*, XII, p. 136
8.	Kedarpur	CP	Śrīcandra	*EI*, XVII, p. 188
9.	Dhulia	CP	Śrīcandra	*EI*, XXIII, p.134
10.	Edilpur	CP	Śrīcandra	*EI*, XVII, p. 189
11.	Dhāka	CP	Kalyaṇacandra	*PIHC*, 23, Part I, p. 36
12.	Bhārellā	Image	Ladahacandra	*EI*, XVIII, p. 349
13.	Maināmati	CP (2)	Ladahacandra	*PIHC*, 23, Part I, p. 36
14.	Maināmati	CP	Govindacandra	*Ibid.*
15.	Kulkudi	Image	Govindacandra	*EI*, XXVII, p.24
16.	Vetkā	Image	Govindacandra	*EI*, XXVII, p.26
17.	Belāva	CP	Bhojavarman	*EI*, XII, p. 37
18.	Samantasar	CP	Harivarman	*EI*, XXX, p.255

19.	Bhubanesvar	CP	Harivarman (Bhaṭṭa Bhavadeva)	*EI*, VI, p. 88
20.	Vajrayogini	CP	Samalavarman	*EI*, XXX, p. 259
21.	Irdā	CP	Nayapāla	*EI*, XXII, p.150
22.	Bāngarh (Dinājpur)	Pillar	Kunjaraghaṭāvarṣa	*JASB*, N.S. VII, p. 619
23.	Kamāuli	CP	Vaidyadeva	*EI*, II, p. 350
24.	Gayā	Temple	Yakṣapāla	*IA*, XVI, p. 63
25.	Gayā	Image	Paritoṣa	*EI*, XXXVI, p.88
26.	Rāmganj	CP	Iśvaraghoṣa	*IB*, p. 149
27.	Mаināmati	CP	Ranavankamalla	*IHQ*, IX, p. 282

B. (I) Epigraphic records of the Bhaumakara dynasty in Orissa

S. No	*Locality*	*Material*	*King or Queen*	*References*
* 1.	Neulpur	CP	Śubhakaradeva	*EI*, XV, (1919-20) pp. 1-8
2.	Caurāsī	CP	Śivakaradeva	*JBORS*, XIV, iii (1928) pp. 292-306
3.	Ganeśa Gumphā	Stone	Śāntikaradeva's time	*EI*, XIII, (12) (1915-16), p. 167
4.	Dhauli Cave	Stone	Śāntikaradeva's time	*EI*, XIX, (1927-28), pp. 263-64
5.	Terundia	CP	Śubhakaradeva	*EI*, XXVIII, (1949-50), pp. 211-16
6.	Hindol	CP	Śubhakaradeva	*JBORS*, XVI, (1930) pp. 69-83
7.	Dharākoṭe	CP	Śubhakaradeva	*JAHRS*, IV, iii & iv (1930) pp. 89-194.
8.	Dhenkanāl	CP	Tribhuvana Mahādevī	*JBORS* II, iv (1916) pp. 419-27
9.	Tālcher	CP	Śubhakaradeva	B. Mishra, *Orissa under the Bhauma Kings* 1934, pp. 32-39

S. No	Locality	Material	King or Queen	References
10.	Tālcher	CP	Śivakaradeva	*Ibid.*, pp. 40-50
11.	Tālcher	CP	Śivakaradeva	*Ibid.*, p. 51
12.	Boud (2)	CP	Tribhuvana Mahādevī	EI, XXIX, (1951-52) pp. 210-20
13.	Gaṅjam	CP	Daṇḍī Mahādevī	*EI*, VI (1900-01) pp. 133-40
14.	Gaṅjam	CP	Daṇḍī Mahādevī	*Ibid.*, pp. 140-42
15.	Sāntigrāma	CP	Daṇḍī Mahādevī	*EI*, XXIX, (1951-52), pp. 79-89
16.	Kumurang	CP	Daṇḍī Mahādevī	*JBORS*, V, iv, (1919) pp. 564-77
17.	Ambāgaon	CP	Daṇḍī Mahādevī	Unpublished
18.	Arual	CP	Daṇḍī Mahādevī	Unpublished
19.	—	CP	Vakula Mahādevī	*EI*, XXXVI, (1966) pp. 307-12
20.	Angul	CP	Dharma Mahādevī	Mishra, *op. cit.* pp. 52-56
21.	Talatalai	CP	Dharma Mahādevi	*IHQ*, XXI, iii (1945) pp. 213-22
22.	Khadipaḍā	Stone Image	Śubhakaradeva's time	*EI*, XXVI (1941-42) pp. 247-48
23.	Hamsesvara	Stone Temple	Śubhakaradeva's time	*EI*, XXVIII (1949-50) pp. 181-83
24.	Cāmuṇḍia	Stone Image	Vatsadevī	*Ibid.*, pp. 184-85
25.	Angul	CP	—	*OHRJ*, XIII, iv, pp. 1-4.

(II) Inscriptions of the Feudatories of the Bhaumakaras

(a) SULKIS

S. No.	*Locality*	*Material*	*Name of the ruler*	*Reference*
1.	Dhenkanāl	CP	Jayastambha	*JBORS* II, pp. 405-09
2.	Purī	CP	Ranastambha	*JASB*, XLIV, (1895) pp. 123-27
3.	Dhenkanāl	CP	Ranastambha	*JBORS*, II pp. 396-400
4.	Tālcher	CP	Kulastambha	*EI*, XII, pp. 156-58
5.	Dhenkanāl	CP	Kulastambha	*JBORS*, II, pp. 400-05
6.	Hindol	CP	Kulastambha	*EI*, XXVIII, pp. 107, 114
7.	Dhenkanāl	CP	Jayastambha	*JBORS*, II, pp. 412-17
8.	Dhenkanāl	CP	Nidayastambha	*JBORS*, II, pp. 409-12

(b) TUNGAS

1.	Bonai	CP	Vinitatuṅga	*JBORS*, VI, pp. 238-40
2.	Khargaprasad	CP	Vinitatuṅga	*OHRJ*, XI No. 4, pp. 242-52
3.	Tālcher	CP	Vinitatuṅga II	*EI*, XXXVIII, pp. 128-31
4.	Tālcher (2)	CP	Gayadatuṅga	*JASB*, V (1909) pp. 347-50, *EI*, XXXIV, pp. 96-100

(c) NANDODBHAVAS

1.	Jayapur	CP	Devanandadeva	*JBORS*, XV, pp. 87-97
2.	Bāripadā	CP (Museum)	Devanandadeva	*EI*, XXVI, pp. 74-78
3.	Narasiṁhapur	CP	Devanandadeva	*EI*, XXVII, pp. 331-36
4.	Dasapallā	CP	Devanandadeva	*EI*, XXIX, pp. 183-89

(d) BHAÑJAS OF KHIÑJALI MAṆḌALA

1.	Dasapallā	CP	Ranabhañja	*JBORS*, VI, pp. 269-73
2.	Tesapaikera	CP	Ranabhañja	*JBORS*, II, pp. 167-77

S. No.	*Locality*	*Material*	*Name of the ruler*	*Reference*
3.	Simghara	CP	Ranabhañja	*JBORS*, VI, pp. 481-86
4.	Baud	CP	Ranabhañja	*EI*, XII, pp. 322-28
5.	Baud	CP	Kanakabhañja	*JBORS*, VI, pp. 356-74
6.	Baud	CP	Solanbhaañja	*JBORS*, VI, pp. 266-73
7.	Sonepur	CP	Śatrubhañja	*EI*, XI, pp. 99-101
8.	Gaṅjam	CP	Śatrubhañja	*OHRJ*, V, No. 3-4 pp. 67-74
9.	Dasapallā	CP	Śatrubhañja	*OHRJ*, I, No. 3, pp. 208
10.	Gaṅjam	CP	Vidyādharabhañja	*EI*, XVIII, pp. 296-98
11.	Antirigam	CP	Yaśabhañja	*EI*, XVIII, pp. 298-99
12.	Antirigam	CP	Jayabhañja	*EI*, XIX, pp. 41-45
(e) NALAS				
1.	Pandiapathara	CP	Bhimasena	*OHRJ*, VI, pp. 97-101

(III) Inscriptions of the Contemporary dynasties

S. No	*Locality*	*Material*	*Name of the Ruler*	*Reference*
(a) RĀṢṬRAKŪṬAS				
1.	Sanjan	CP	Amoghavarṣa	*EI*, XVIII, pp. 235 ff.
2.	Daśāvatāra, Ellorā	Cave Ins.	—	*ASWI*, v, p. 92
(b) PĀLAS				
1.	Monghyr	CP	Devapāla	*IA*, XXI, pp. 255 ff.
2.	Bhāgalpur	CP	Nārāyaṇapāla	*IA*, XV, pp. 304 ff.
3.	Bādāl	Pillar	Nārāyaṇapāla	*EI*, II, pp. 165 ff.
(c) SOMAVAṀŚĪS				
1.	Khadiparā	CP	Dharmaratha	*OHRJ*, XII, No. 2, pp. 62 ff.

2.	Bānapur	CP	Indraratha	*JAS*, VIII, No. 4, pp. 272 ff.
3.	Mallar	CP	Mahāśivagupta	*EI*, XXIII, pp. 113 ff.
4.	—	CP	Bhimaratha	*EI*, III, pp. 355 ff.

(d) NEPAL

1.	Pasupati Temple	Stone	—	*IA*, IX, pp. 179 ff.
2.	Baragāon	CP	Ratnapālavarman	*JASB*, LXVII, pp. 99 ff.
3.	Hayungthal	CP	Harjavarman	*Kāmarūpa, Sāsanāvali*, ed. by P. Bhattacharya, pp. 48 ff.

Select Bibliography

PRIMARY SOURCES

(i) Inscriptions *

De, S. C., *Descriptive Catalogue of the Copper Plate Inscriptions of Orissa*, Bhopal, 1961.

Fleet, J.F., *Corpus Inscriptionum Indicarum* (Vol. III); *Inscriptions of the Early Gupta Kings and their Successors*, Calcutta, 1888.

Hultzsch, E., *South Indian Inscriptions* (3 Vols.), Madras, 1890-1929.

Maitreya, Akshaya Kumar, *Gauda-lekhamala*, Rājaśāhī, 1912.

Majumdar, N.G., *Inscriptions of Bengal* (Vol. III), Rājaśāhī, 1929.

Mukherji, Ramaranjan and Maity S.K., *Corpus of Bengal Inscriptions,* Calcutta 1967.

Rajguru, S.N., *Inscriptions of Orissa* (Vols. I, II, IV), Bhubanesvar, 1958-66.

Sircar, D.C., *Select Inscriptions bearing on Indian History and Civilization* (Vol. I), Calcutta, 1965.

(ii) Coins

Chakraborty, S.K., *A study of Ancient Indian Numismatics*, Mymen Singh, 1931.

*List of Inscriptions is given separately in this publication.

Smith, V., *A Catalogue of Coins in the Indian Museum* (Vol. I), Calcutta, Oxford, 1906.

(iii) Literature

A. Foreign Texts

(a) *Chinese*

Beal, Samuel (tr.), *Life of Hiuen Tsiang by S.H. Li*, London, 1911.

———, (tr.), *Si-yu-ki, Buddhist Records of the Western World* (2 Vols.), London, 1906.

Giles, H. A. (tr.), *The Travels of Fa-Hien*, Cambridge, 1923.

Legge, J. (tr.), *Fahien's Record of Buddhistic Kingdoms,* Oxford, 1886.

Takakusu, J. (tr.), *I-tsing—A record of the Buddhist Religion as practised in India and the Malaya Archipelago*, Oxford, 1896.

Watters, T. (tr.), *On Yuan Chwang's Travels in India*, London, 1904-5.

(b) *Tibetan*

Chattopadhyay, D.P. (tr.), *History of Buddhism in India by Lama Taranatha*, Calcutta, 1970.

Das, S.C. (ed.), *PAG-SAM-JON-ZANG by Sumpa Mkhampo*, Calcutta, 1908.

Dutta, B.N. (ed.), *Mystic Tales of Lama Taranatha*, Calcutta, 1944.

(c) *Persian and Arabic*

Elliot, H.M. and Dowson, J., *The History of India as told by its own Historian* (Vol. I), London, 1870.

Minorsky, V. (ed.), *Hudud-al-Alam or Regions of the World*, Oxford, 1937.

B. Indigenous

Ānandāśrama Sanskrit Series (ed.)., *Matsya Purāṇa*. Poona, 1907.

Bagchi, P.C. (ed.), *Caryapādas*. Journal of the Deptt. of Letters, Calcutta Univeristy, (Vol. XXVIII).

Bhattacharya (ed.), *Sādhanamālā* (2 Vols.), Calcutta, 1925-28.

Ganapati-Sastri, T. (ed.)., *Arya Manjusri Mulakalpa* (3 parts), Trivandrum, 1920-25.

Kashyap, B.J. (ed.), *Aṅguttara Nikāya*, I, 1960.

Kinjawadekar, R. (ed.), *Harivaṁśa-Purāṇa* Poona, 1936.

Law, B.C. (ed.), *Daṭhavaṁsa*, Lahore, 1925.

Mitra, R.L. (ed.), *Aṣṭasāhasrika-Prajnāpāramitā*, Calcutta, 1888.

Pargiter, F.E. (tr.), *Mārkaṇḍeya Purāṇa*, Calcutta, 1904.

Prachi Samiti (published). *Mādalā Pānji*, Cuttack, 1940.

Rhys Davids, T.W. (tr.), *Majjhima Nikāya*, Oxford, 1881.

Sanyal, J.M. (tr.), *Bhāgavata Purāṇa*, Calcutta, 1952.

Sastri, H.P. (ed.). *Rāmacarita of Sandhyākara Nandi*, Calcutta, 1910.

Shama Sastri, K. (ed.), *Arthaśāstra*, Mysore, 1929.

SECONDARY SOURCES

Books

Acharya, P., *Studies in Orissan History, Archaeology and Archieves*, Cuttack, 1969.

Agarwala, V.S., *Matsya Purāṇa, a study*, Varanasi, 1963.

Ahir, D.C., *India's Debt to Buddhism*, New Delhi, 1964.

Altekar, A.S., *Education in Ancient India,* Benares, 1957.

———, *State and Government in Ancient India*, Delhi, 1958.

Bagchi, P. C., *Dohākośa*, Calcutta, 1938.

———, *Studies in the Tantras* (part 1), Calcutta, 1975 (second impression).

Banerji, R.D., *History of Orissa*. (Vol. I & II), Calcutta, 1930-31.

———, *The Pālas of Bengal*, Calcutta, 1915.

Barya, K.L., *Early History of Kāmarūpa*, Shillong, 1933.

Basak, R.G., *The History of North-Eastern India*, Calcutta, 1967.

Basham, A.L., *The wonder that was India*, London, 1982.

Bhattacharya, Benoytosh, *An Introduction to Buddhist Estoterism*, Oxford, 1932, reprint, Benaras, 1964.

Bhattacharya, H., *Cultural Heritage of India*, Calcutta, 1969.

Bhattacharya, N.N., *History of Researches in Indian Buddhism*, Delhi, 1981.

Bhattasali, N.K., *Iconography of Buddhist and Brahmanical sculptures in the Dacca Museum*, Dacca, 1929.

Bhogowalia, V., *Vaishnavism and society in Northern India*, Delhi, 1980.

Bose, P.N., *Indian Teachers of Buddhist Universities,* Madras, 1923.

Brown, Percy, *Indian Architecture* (Vol. I), Bombay, 1971.

———, *A Guide to the Principal interest in Orissa*, Calcutta, 1900.

Burgess, James, *Ancient Monuments, Temples and Sculptures of India*, (2 Vols.), London, 1897.

Chanda, R.P., *Medieval Indian Sculptures in the British Museum*, London, 1936.

Chattarji, S.K., *The place of Assam in the History and Civilization of India*, Gauhati, 1955.

Chattopadhyaya, Debi Prasad (ed.), *History and Society (Essays in the Honour of Prof. Niharranjan Roy)*, Calcutta, 1976.

Chattopadhyay, S., *Early History of Northern India*, Calcutta, 1958.

———, *Social Life in Ancient India*, Calcutta, 1965.

Chaudhury, P.C., *The History of Civilization of the People of Assam*, Gauhati, 1966.

Chaudhury, A.M., *Dynastic History of Bengal*, Dacca, 1967.

Chaudhury, B.N., *Buddhist Centres in Ancient India*, Calcutta, 1969.

Chaudhury, P.C., Cobden-Ramsay, L.E.B., *Bengal Gazetters, Gazetter of Feudatory* States *of Orissa*, Howrah, 1950.

Coomaraswamy, A.K., *Elements of Buddhist Iconography*, London, 1934.

Cunningham, Alexander, *Mahabodhi*, London, 1891.

Das, Bhaskar, *Social and Economic Life of Southern Orissa*, Calcutta, 1985.

Das, Biswasrupa, *The Bhaumakaras — Buddhist Kings of Orissa and Their Times*, Delhi, 1978.

———, *Orissa — Social, Cultural and Religious Aspects*, Delhi, 1985.

Das, Binod Sarkar, *Economic History of Orissa*, Calcutta, 1978.

———, *Life and Culture in Orissa*, Calcutta, 1984.

Das, D., *The Early History of Kalinga*, Calcutta, 1977.

Das, H.C., *Cultural Developments in Orissa*, Calcutta, 1985.

Das, M.N. (ed.), *Sidelines on History and Culture of Orissa*, Cuttack, 1978.

———, *Glimpses of Kalinga History*, Calcutta 1949.

Dasgupta, K.K. (ed.), *Fleet's Topographical List of the Brihat-Samhita*, Calcutta, 1973.

Datta, B.N. (tr.), *Mystic Tales of Lama Taranatha*, Calcutta, 1944.

Davids, T.W. Rhys, *Buddhism, Its History and Literature*, New edition, London, 1926.

De, S.C., *Descriptive Catalogue of the Copper Plate Inscriptions of Orissa*, Bhubanesvar, 1961.

Dutt, Nalinaksha, *Aspects of Mahayana Buddhism and its Relation to Hinayana*, London, 1930.

———, *Early Monastic Buddhism*, Vol. I, Calcutta, 1941.

Dutta, Sukumar, *Buddhist Monks and Monasteries of India*, London, 1962.

Eliot, Charter, *Hinduism and Buddhism*, (Vols. I-III), London, 1921, reprint, 1954.

French, J.C., *The Art of the Pala Empire in Bengal*, Oxford, 1928.

Gait, E.A., *A History of Assam*, Calcutta, 1906.

Ganguli, D.K., *The Agrarian System in Ancient India*, Calcutta, 1930.

———, *Historical Geography and Dynastic History of Orissa*, Calcutta, 1975.

Ganguli, M.M., *Orissa and Her Remains*, Calcutta, 1912.

Ghosh, A., *A Guide to Nalanda*, New Delhi, 1965.

Ghosh, N.N., *Early History of India*, Allahabad, 1951.

Ghoshal, U.N., *A contribution to the History of Hindu Revenue System*, Calcutta, 1929.

Haig, Sir Wolseley, *Combridge History of India*, (Vol. III), Cambridge, 1928.

Haldar, J., *Social Life in Ancient India*, Calcutta.

Hastings, J. (ed.), *Encyclopaedia of Religion and Ethics*, Edinburgh, 1915.

Hazra, Kanailal, *Royal Patronage of Buddhism in Ancient India,* Delhi, 1984.

Hultzsch, E., *Corpus Inscriptionum Indicarum* (Vol. I), Oxford, 1925.

Hussain, Sahanara, *Everyday Life in Pāla Empire*, Dacca, 1968.

Jha, D.N., *Ancient India — An Introductory Outline,* New Delhi, 1983.

Joshi, Lalmani, *Studies in the Buddhistic Culture in India*, Delhi, 1967.

Kane, P.V., *History of Dharmasastra* (Vols I-V). Poona, 1930-62.

Karmarkar, A.P., *The Religions of India* (Vol. I), Lonavala, 1950.

Keith, A.B., *A History of Sanskrit Literature*, Oxford, 1928.

Kramrisch, Stella, *Indian Sculpture*, Calcutta, 1933.

———, *Pāla and Sena Sculpture*, 1929.

Kulke, Herman (ed.) (in collaboration with G. Dash, Manmathnath Das and K.S. Behra), *Orissa, A Comprehensive and classified Bibliography*, Cuttack, 1951.

Law, B.C., *Historical Geography of Ancient India*, Paris, 1954.

Law, N.N., *Aspects of Ancient Indian Polity*, Oxford, 1921.

Mahtab, H., *The History of Orissa*, (Vol. I), Cuttack, 1959.

———, *Odisara Itihasa* (Oriya), Cuttack, 1948.

Maity, S.K., *Economic Life of North India in the Gupta Period*, Calcutta, 1957.

Majumdar, Gayātri Sen, *Buddhism in Bengal*, Calcutta, 1983.

Majumdar, R.C. *Ancient India*, Benaras, 1952.

———, *Outline of the History of Kalinga*, Dacca, 1938-39.

——— (ed.)., *The History of Bengal*, (Vol. I) *Hindu Period*, Dacca, 1943.

——— (ed.), *History and Culture of Indian People,* (Vol. IV) *Age of Imperial Kanauj,* Bombay, 1955.

———,(Vol.V) *Struggle for Empire,* Bombay, 1957.

———, *History of Ancient Bengal*, Calcutta, 1972.

Majumdar, R.C. and Dasgupta, K.K. (ed.), *Comprehensive History of India*, (Vol. III), New Delhi, 1981-82.

Mazumdar, B. Prasad, *Socio-Economic History of Northern India*, Calcutta, 1960.

Mishra, Binayak, *Dynasties of Medieval Orissa*, Calcutta, 1933.

———, *Orissa under the Bhauma Kings*, Calcutta 1934.

Mishra, K.C., *The Cult of Jagannatha*, Calcutta, 1971.

Mitra, Debala, *Buddhist Monuments*, Calcutta, 1971.

———, *Ratnagiri*, (2 Vols), New Delhi, 1981-83.

Mitra, R.C., *Decline of Buddhism in India*, Visvabharati, 1954.

Mitra, R.L., *Antiquities of Orissa* (2 Vols), Calcutta, 1875.

Mittal, A.C., *An Early History of Orissa*, Benares, 1962.

Mohapatra, R.P., *Archaeology in Orissa*, (Vol. I), Delhi, 1986.

Morrison, B.M., *Political Centres and Cultural Regions in Early Bengal*, Arizona, 1970.

Mudgal, B.S., *Political Economy in Ancient India*, Kanpur, 1960.

Mukherjee, P., *The History of Medieval Vaishnavism in Orissa*, Calcutta, 1940.

Mukherjee, Sandhya, *Some Aspects of Social Life in Ancient India*, Allahabad, 1976.

Mukherjee, R.K., *Ancient India*, Allahabad, 1956.

Nandi, R.N., *Social Roots of Religion in Ancient India*, Delhi, 1987.

Panigrahi, K.C., *Bhauma Art and Architecture*, Madras, 1961.

———, *Chronology of the Bhaumankaras and Somavamsis of Orissa*, Madras, 1961.

———, *History of Orissa*, Cuttack, 1981.

Paul, P.L., *The Early History of Bengal*, (2 Vols.), Calcutta, 1939-40.

Pillai, L.D.S., *An Indian Ephemeris* (Vol. I, Pt. I), Madras, 1922.

Prasad, Beni, *The State in Ancient India*, Allahabad.

Rajguru, S.N., *History of the Gangas*, Government of Orissa, 1972.

———, *Inscriptions of Orissa* (2 Vols.), Government of Orissa, 1958-60.

Rath, A.K., *Studies on Some Aspects of the History and Culture of Orissa*, Calcutta, 1982.

Rath, B.K., *Cultural History of Orissa*, Delhi, 1981.

Ray, H.C., *Dynastic History of Northern India*, (Vol. I), Calcutta, 1931.

Ray Chaudhuri, H.C., *Political History of Ancient India*, Calcutta, 1938.

———, *Studies in Indian Antiquities*, Calcutta, 1959.

Risley, H.H.,*Tribes and Castes of Bengal* (2 Vols.), Calcutta, 1890, 1892.

Roerich, Nicholas, *Blue Annals*, Calcutta, 1948.

Sahu, N.K., *Buddhism in Orissa*, Utkal University, 1958.

———, *History of Orissa* (Vol. I), Utkal University, 1964.

———, (ed.), *New Aspects of History of Orissa*, Sambalpur, 1971.

Saraswati, S.K., *Early Sculpture of Bengal*, Calcutta, 1962.

Sen, B.C., *Some Historical Aspects of the Inscriptions of Bengal*, Calcutta, 1942.

Sengupta, Sudha, *Buddhism in the Classical Age*, Delhi, 1985.

Shah, A.P., *Life in Medieval Orissa*, Varanasi, 1976.

Sharma, R.S., *Aspects of Political Ideas and Institutions in Ancient India*. Delhi, 1959.

——— (ed.), *Indian Society, Historical Probings, in Memory of D.D. Kosambi*, New Delhi, 1974.

———, *Prospectives in Social and Economic History of Early India*, Delhi, 1983.

Shastri, R.S., *Indian Feudalism c 300-1200*, Calcutta 1965.

Sircar, D.C., *Studies in the Geography of Ancient and Medieval India*, Varanasi, 1960.

———, *Indian Epigraphy*, Delhi, 1965.

———, *Select Inscriptions bearing on Indian History and Civilization* (Vol. I), Calcutta, 1942.

———, *Studies in Society and Administration as Ancient and Medieval India* (Vol. I), Calcutta, 1967.

Smith, V.A., *A History of Fine Art in India and Ceylon*, Oxford, 1911.

———, *The Early History of India*, Oxford, 1967.

Subudhi, V., *The Bhaumakaras of Orissa*, Calcutta, 1978.

Thakur, V., *Some Aspects of Ancient Indian History and Culture*, New Delhi, 1974.

Thapar, R., *A History of India*, (Vol. I), London, 1969.

Tripathy, R.S., *History of Kanauj to the Muslim Conquest*, Delhi, 1959.

Vasu, N.N., *The Archaeological Survey of Mayurbhanj*, Calcutta, 1911.

———, *The Social History of Kamarupa*, (Vol. III), Calcutta, 1933.

Vaidya, C.V., *Epic India*, Bombay, 1933.

Waddel, L.A., *The Buddhism of Tibet or Lamaism*, London, 1890.

Wagle, N.C., *Society at the Time of Buddha*, Bombay, 1968.

Warder, A.K., *Indian Buddhism*, Delhi, 1970.

Winternitz, M., *History of Indian Literature*, (Vol. II), Calcutta, 1933.

Zimmer, Heinrich, *Art of Indian Asia*, (2 Vols.), New York, 1955.

Journals and Periodicals

Ancient India (Bulletin of Archaeological Survey of India), Delhi.

Annals of the Bhandarkar Oriental Research Institute, Poona.

Annual Report of the A.S.I, Published by Government of India.

Asiatic Researches, Calcutta.

Calcutta Review, Calcutta.

Diganta (Oriya), Cuttack.

Epigraphica Indica, Published by Government of India.

Indian Antiquary, Bombay, Calcutta.

Indian Culture, Calcutta.

Indian Historical Quarterly, Calcutta.

Jhankāra (Oriya), Cuttack.

Journal of the Andhra Historical Research Society, Rajahmundry.

Journal of the Asiastic Society, Calcutta.

Journal of the Asiastic Society of Bengal, Calcutta.

Journal of the Asiastic Society, Letters; Calcutta.

Journal of the Bihar and Orissa Research Society, Patna.

Journal of the Indian History, Trivendrum.

Journal of the Kalinga Historical Research Society, Balangir.

Journal of the Numismatic Society of India, Calcutta.

Journal of the Peasant Studies, Delhi.

Journal of the Oriental Research, Madras.

Journal of the Orissa Academy, Cuttack.

Journal of the Royal Asiastic Society, London.

Mahabodhi, Mahabodhi Society of India, Varanasi.

Memoirs of the Archaeological Śurvey of India, Calcutta.

Modern Review, Calcutta.

Orissa Historical Research Journal, Government of Orissa, Bhubanesvar.

Proceedings of the All India, Published from different places.

Proceedings of the Indian History Congress, Published from different places.

Glossary

Ācārya : learned teacher.

Anāgāmī : a state of a Buddhist monk (Theravādin concept).

Anuloma : a type of Hindu marriage where the caste of the bridegroom is higher than that of the bride.

Arhat : the highest stage of a Buddhist monk, free from desire (Theravādin concept).

Avalokiteśvara : a Bodhisattva (Potential Buddha) who took birth before Buddha (*Mahāyāna* concept).

Baiśākha : an Indian month.

Bhukti : old name of district.

Bhūmisparśamūdrā : posture of touching the earth by Buddha.

Caitya : Buddhist temple for meditation.

Cāmuṇḍā : a form of Durgā, a Hindu goddess.

Caryāpadas : Buddhist mystic songs.

Deva : Gods of Brāhmaṇism.

Devācikā upāsaka : devotee of the two precepts of Buddhism (Buddha and *Dharma*) before the formation of *Saṁgha*.

Dhāraṇī : protective magical formula, used by Tāntric Buddhists.

Dohās : stanzas.

Heruka : a *Vajrayāna* Buddhist deity.

Homa : oblation given to fire-god.

Jambhala : a *Vajrayāna* Buddhist deity.

Janakabhuh : ancestral home.

Jaṭāmukuṭa : a Bodhisattva with matted hair.

Kātyāyani : a form of Durgā, a Hindu goddess.

Kāvya: poem.

Madhyadeśa : areas of the central part of the country (India).

Mahāsāṅghika : precursur of Mahāyānists.

Maitreya : the future Buddha, a Bodhisattva also.

Mañjuśrī : a Bodhisattva who took birth before Buddha.

Mārici: Buddhist Sun God.

Mitrika : mother.

Mleccha : out-caste.

Padmapāṇi : a form of *avalokiteśvara*; a Bodhisattva having lotus on his head.

Paramabhaṭṭāraka : title taken by Hindu kings.

Parama saugata : a devout disciple of Buddha.

Pātaka : a unit of land measurement.

Prajñāpāramitā : the last of the six perfectionary virtues obtained by the Bodhisattva, a *Vajrayāna* goddess.

Prakṛti : subjects.

Praśasti : eulogy.

Pratiloma : a type of Hindu marriage where the caste of the bridegroom is lower than that of the bride.

Puṇḍit : proficient in knowledge.

Purāṇa : religious book.

Rājabhaṭādivamsa patita : an inscription dealing with the genealogy of the Pālas of Bengal.

Sakadagāmī : Theravādin Buddhist concept of the stage of a monk.

Sammiteya : a sect of Sthaviravādin Buddhism.

Samudra : ocean.

Sarvāṇī image : a form of Brāhmaṇical goddess Durgā.

Sarvastivādin : an old form of Buddhism.

Siddhācāryas : great teachers.

Siddhi : achievement.

Śloka : verses.

Smārta : a Brāhmaṇic ritual done according to the *Smṛti* texts.

Smṛti : memory.

Sotāpanna : Thereavādin Buddhist concept of stage of a monk.

Śrauta : a Brāhmaṇic ritual done according to the *Smṛti* texts.

Śrāvaka : lay devotees of Buddha.

Śruti : revelation.

Sthaviravādin or *Theravādin* : the most orthodox school of early Buddhism.

Stūpa : place of worship of the Buddhists.

Sugata : Buddha.

Thera : a senior monk.

Tirthikas : heretics.

Upāsaka : lay male disciple of Buddha.

Upāsikā : lay female disciple of Buddha.

Utkala kula : family of Utkala or Orissa.

Vajrasattva : a *Vajrayāna* Buddhist deity.

Vāṅgiya Sāhitya Pariṣad : a literary organisation of Bengal.

Varṇa-saṅkara : mixed caste.

Varṇāśrama : caste system.

Vasudhana : a *Vajrayāna* Buddhist deity.

Virajākṣetra : the land of Hindu goddess Virajā (Jājpur in Orissa).

Yakṣa : a Hindu demigod, who protects the temples.

Index

Fig. 1. Buddha, Achyutarajpur, Orissa.

Fig. 2. Bodhisattva Mañjuśrī,
Achyutarajpur, Orissa.

Fig. 3. Tārā, Achyutarajpur, Orissa.

Fig. 4. Votive Stūpa, Achyutarajpur, Orissa.

Fig. 5. Tārā, Mangalpur, Orissa.

Fig. 6.Tārā, Nimapara, Orissa.

Fig. 7. Bodhisattva Vajrapāṇi, Lalitagiri, Orissa.

Fig. 8. Bodhisattva Padmapāṇi, Orissa.

Fig. 9. Śākyamuni Buddha, Chaudwar, Orissa.

Fig. 10. Bust of Buddha, stone, Ratnagiri, Orissa.

Fig. 11. Buddha in *Bhūmisparśa Mudrā*, Ratnagiri, Orissa.

Fig. 12. Buddha in *Dhyāna Mudrā*, Ratnagiri, Orissa.

Fig. 13. Māyādevī, Birth of Buddha, Nalanda, Bihar.

Fig. 14. Crowned Buddha, Bihar.

Fig. 15. Tārā, Bodh Gaya, Bihar.

Fig. 16. Tārā, Bihar.

Fig. 17. Some aspects of Buddha's life, Bihar.

Fig. 18. Buddha in Preaching pose, Eastern India.

Fig. 19. *Aṣṭa Mahābodhisattvas*, Bengal.

Fig. 20. *Dhyānī* Buddha, Bihar.

Fig. 21. Buddha Panel, Bengal.